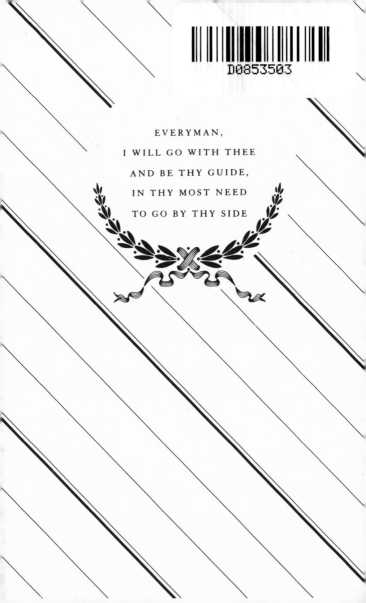

EVERYMAN,
I WILL GO WITH THEE
AND BE THY GUIDE,
IN THY MOST NEED
TO GO BY THY SIDE

EVERYMAN'S LIBRARY
POCKET POETS

THE FOUR
SEASONS

POEMS

••••••••••••••••••

EDITED BY

J. D. McCLATCHY

EVERYMAN'S LIBRARY
POCKET POETS

Alfred A. Knopf New York London Toronto

THIS IS A BORZOI BOOK
PUBLISHED BY ALFRED A. KNOPF

This selection by J. D. McClatchy first published in
Everyman's Library, 2008
Copyright © 2008 by Everyman's Library
Foreword Copyright © 2008 by J. D. McClatchy

A list of acknowledgments to copyright owners appears at the back
of this volume.

All rights reserved. Published in the United States by Alfred A. Knopf,
a division of Random House, Inc., New York, and in Canada by Random
House of Canada Limited, Toronto. Distributed by Random House, Inc.,
New York. Published in the United Kingdom by Everyman's Library,
Northburgh House, 10 Northburgh Street, London EC1V 0AT.
Distributed by Random House (UK) Ltd.

US website: www.randomhouse.com/everymans

ISBN 978-0-307-26834-1 (US)
978-1-84159-781-2 (UK)

A CIP catalogue record for this book is available from the British Library

Library of Congress Cataloging-in-Publication Data
The four seasons: poems / edited by J. D. McClatchy.
p. cm.—(Everyman's Library pocket poets)
Includes index.
ISBN-13: 978-0-307-26834-1 (alk. paper)
1. Seasons—Poetry. 2. English poetry. 3. American poetry.
I. McClatchy, J. D., 1945–.
PR1195.S42F68 2008   2008003014
821′.008′033—dc22

Typography by Peter B. Willberg
Typeset in the UK by AccComputing, North Barrow, Somerset
Printed and bound in Germany by GGP Media GmbH, Pössneck

CONTENTS

9

2

FOREWORD

The seasons are both segments of time and states of mind. Though our word "season" derives from the Latin for "sowing" and refers thereby only to spring, every culture has had terms – whether winter and summer, or rainy and dry – for the sequence of great climatic changes by which the world transforms itself every year. But it's more than what is going on outside. Our hearts have seasons as well. Mostly, we call them moods, and we lay our plans by their accustomed recurrences. We recall the crucial moments in our lives by the weather that still swirls around them in memory. Weddings and family reunions, getaways and homecomings are most often scheduled by the season. Yes, we have urgent appointments and traditional holidays, our deadlines and habits. But our bodies and their tides of desire seem to move more slowly, and are governed by the larger, more dramatic and decisive movements of the sun itself – the arrival of light and the opulence of warmth, then their slow fading and cold withdrawal. Aren't, in fact, the seasons like the stages of a love affair?

This is where the poets come in. They are enthusiasts and brooders. Love and death are their stock-in-trade. But first of all, they are observers. A strong imagination begins with a keen eye. The poet is interested in both the detail and the scheme, in both the streak on the tulip and the nature of beauty which the flower represents. This is why the seasons have, down the centuries, had a special appeal for poets. (It's interesting though obvious to note that modern poets from England and especially from New England, where weather patterns are more extreme, are more likely to write about the seasons than poets from more steadily temperate parts.) This book is a virtual anthology of small details, because the seasons invite us to catalogue the terms of our love for the world. It takes hours of observation to get the tiniest half-line right that describes, say, the precise shade of a bird's wing in flight. And such details are then the starting-point of metaphor. We can't see anything exactly as it is unless we first see it as something else. The poet Howard Nemerov offers an instructive example:

While I am thinking about metaphor, a flock of purple finches arrives on the lawn. Since I haven't seen these birds for some years, I am only fairly sure of their being in fact purple finches, so I get down Peterson's *Field Guide* and read his description: "Male: About the size of House Sparrow, rosy-red, brightest on head and rump." That checks quite well, but his next remark – "a sparrow dipped in raspberry juice" – is decisive: it fits. I look out the window again, and now I *know* that I am seeing purple finches.

* * *

Because the canvas of the four seasons is so large, the pages of this book are filled with an extraordinary range of natural observation and startling imagery. Having lavished this kind of attention on a poem, the poet then wants to implicate something beyond the transient hold of a season. When Robert Frost, for instance, says that "Nature's first green is gold," he is saying two things at once: that the first faint wash of color on a stand of trees in early spring is paradoxically of a yellowish tint, and that the arrival of spring is, for all its precariousness, of inestimable value.

If winter comes, can spring be far behind? It is often the case – how could it be otherwise? – that poems about one season include a memory or an anticipation of an adjacent season. That is the way the mind works, one image overlapping another, one sensation dissolving into its opposite. At other times, the season's bounty may function as an ironic counterpart to the speaker's situation. In William Carlos Williams's "The Widow's Lament in Springtime," the flowering world only makes the woman's grief the more piercing: everything in the world is restored but the one thing she wants, her dead husband. Or in Sara Teasdale's "There Will Come Soft Rains," written with the horrors of the First World War in mind, spring seems almost cruel in the way it will burst on us bounteously, like a shell, without regard for any man's wretched condition.

The first glistening bud, the first uncertain robin, the first crack in the pond-ice . . . there is every reason why spring has always been the season of hope. It is not just that it signals a return but that it enacts one of our deepest fantasies: the chance to begin over again. It is the least overwhelming of the seasons because it so closely matches our own feelings, and the poems in the first section of this book are redolent of what Gerard Manley Hopkins rightly calls the juice and joy of "earth's sweet being in the beginning."

Henry James once said that the two most beautiful words in the English language were "summer afternoon." Summer is at least the source of our happiest memories, undoubtedly because of its connections to the carefree innocence of childhood. It is the season that allows us the most direct contact with itself, and perhaps for that reason summer, too, can be literally overwhelming. The glut of the woods and the garden, when every wild creature and cultivated plant appears, marks a time when the merely human is deliciously subordinate to the luxuriance of nature. Everything seems to have reached its richest apogee, and time itself – because an edenic image of perfection is before our eyes – seems to stand still. It is the season of strain, when everything pushes to grow and bloom, yet it is the season of idleness as well.

"The poetry of earth is never dead," writes Keats in

his great sonnet about summer. Yet in his ecstatic praise he drops the hint of death. It is no wonder that autumn is the most poetic of the seasons, leaning back towards summer's green plenty while tipping forward to winter's emptiness. Yes, there is a flamboyant swagger to the turning trees and gusty winds. But of all the seasons, autumn most provokes philosophical meditation, and its poems are more likely to drift from mere description into resonant ideas, to shift from celebration to elegy. It is as if the leaves fall so that we may see through things, look deeply into the mortal process of transformation. There is no more poignant poem in the language than Hopkins's "Spring and Fall," where a young girl is told that the pile of dead leaves before her is an image of the future; there is no more haunting poem in the language than Thomas Hardy's "During Wind and Rain," as a raindrop slips along a name carved on a tombstone. Above all else, the poems in this section of the book express the grave acknowledgment at the heart of our lives: that we too must die. Shakespeare's admonition to "love that well which thou must leave ere long" gives the right twist to the simple phrase *autumn leaves*.

There is nothing brighter than sun on snow, nothing greener than a spruce in January, but in winter the world withers to the outline of itself. It is the season of abstractions, of withholding, of solitude – or, in Wallace

Stevens's chilling words, of the "nothing that is not there and the nothing that is." For all the bleakness of the weather and the bizarreness of the landscape (Emerson called the snowbound view a "frolic architecture"), the consolations of companionship come to the fore, the coziness of the hearth, and the power of dreams. Each of the four seasons is a dream of the others, but none is so intense as winter's. And its perspective is even longer than autumn's. We see ourselves as in a shaken glass globe, safe in the tiny painted house while the handmade storm rages. In Gjertrud Schnackenberg's touching poem "The Paperweight," it is history itself that sifts down on the contained world, and as we watch it all transpire in our palm we learn what it is to stand apart. The world is at its darkest, but at its purest, and the poems winter has inspired have a bracing calm to them, a clarity that only cold allows.

Huai-nan Tzu, the Taoist philosopher who lived in the second century B.C., held that out of nothingness came the Great Beginning which produced the emptiness that in turn produced the universe. Heaven and earth combined became the essential yin and yang of existence, and from those essences came the four seasons, and the scattered essences of the four seasons at last produced all the creatures of the world. It is a fascinating notion to entertain: that we were made of the seasons, that indeed we embody them. We may as well take the next step and say that, out of the seasons we are, our poets have made poems. Call them, too, scattered essences. Each compresses within itself a portion of the years of our lives. Brought together here, they are an illuminated manuscript. The little book now in your hands turns, season by season, around what the mind can make of the world.

J. D. McClatchy

SPRING

FIRST SIGHT OF SPRING

The hazel-blooms, in threads of crimson hue,
Peep through the swelling buds, foretelling Spring,
Ere yet a white-thorn leaf appears in view,
Or March finds throstles pleased enough to sing.
To the old touchwood tree woodpeckers cling
A moment, and their harsh-toned notes renew;
In happier mood, the stockdove claps his wing;
The squirrel sputters up the powdered oak,
With tail cocked o'er his head, and ears erect,
Startled to hear the woodman's understroke;
And with the courage which his fears collect,
He hisses fierce half malice and half glee,
Leaping from branch to branch about the tree,
In winter's foliage, moss and lichens, deckt.

THE YEAR'S AWAKENING

How do you know that the pilgrim track
Along the belting zodiac
Swept by the sun in his seeming rounds
Is traced by now to the Fishes' bounds
And into the Ram, when weeks of cloud
Have wrapt the sky in a clammy shroud,
And never as yet a tint of spring
Has shown in the Earth's apparelling;
      O vespering bird, how do you know,
          How do you know?

How do you know, deep underground,
Hid in your bed from sight and sound,
Without a turn in temperature,
With weather life can scarce endure,
That light has won a fraction's strength,
And day put on some moments' length,
Whereof in merest rote will come,
Weeks hence, mild airs that do not numb,
      O crocus root, how do you know,
          How do you know?

"A LIGHT EXISTS IN SPRING"

A Light exists in Spring
Not present on the Year
At any other period –
When March is scarcely here

A Color stands abroad
On Solitary Fields
That Science cannot overtake
But Human Nature feels.

It waits upon the Lawn,
It shows the furthest Tree
Upon the furthest Slope you know
It almost speaks to you.

Then as Horizons step
Or Noons report away
Without the Formula of sound
It passes and we stay –

A quality of loss
Affecting our Content
As Trade had suddenly encroached
Upon a Sacrament.

EMILY DICKINSON

SPRING

This morning
two birds
fell down the side of the maple tree

like a tuft of fire
a wheel of fire
a love knot

out of control as they plunged through the air
pressed against each other
and I thought

how I meant to live a quiet life
how I meant to live a life of mildness and meditation
tapping the careful words against each other

and I thought –
as though I were suddenly spinning, like a bar of silver
as though I had shaken my arms and *lo!* they were
        wings –

of the Buddha
when he rose from his green garden
when he rose in his powerful ivory body

when he turned to the long dusty road without end
when he covered his hair with ribbons and the petals
   of flowers
when he opened his hands to the world.

"IT WAS A LOVER AND HIS LASS"

It was a lover and his lass,
    With a hey, and a ho, and a hey nonny no,
That o'er the green corn fields did pass
    In spring time, the only pretty ring time,
    When birds do sing, hey ding a ding a ding:
    Sweet lovers love the spring.

Between the acres of the rye,
    With a hey, and a ho, and a hey nonny no,
These pretty country fools would lie,
    In spring time, the only pretty ring time,
    When birds do sing, hey ding a ding a ding:
    Sweet lovers love the spring.

This carol they began that hour,
    With a hey, and a ho, and a hey nonny no,
How that a life was but a flower
    In spring time, the only pretty ring time,
    When birds do sing, hey ding a ding a ding:
    Sweet lovers love the spring.

Then pretty lovers take the time
    With a hey, and a ho, and a hey nonny no,
For love is crownèd with the prime
    In spring time, the only pretty ring time,
    When birds do sing, hey ding a ding a ding:
    Sweet lovers love the spring.

NOTHING GOLD CAN STAY

Nature's first green is gold,
Her hardest hue to hold.
Her early leaf's a flower;
But only so an hour.
Then leaf subsides to leaf.
So Eden sank to grief,
So dawn goes down to day.
Nothing gold can stay.

MARCH

Beech leaves which might have clung
Parching for six weeks more
Were stripped by last night's gale
Which made so black a roar

And drove the snow-streaks level.
So we see in the glare
Of a sun whose white combustion
Cannot warm the air.

From the edge of the woods, in gusts,
The leaves are scuttled forth
Onto a pasture drifted
Like tundras of the north,

To migrate there in dry
Skitter or fluttered brawl,
Then flock into some hollow
Like this, below the wall,

With veins swept back like feathers
To our prophetic sight,
And bodies of gold shadow
Pecking at sparks of light.

SPRING

Nothing is so beautiful as Spring –
    When weeds, in wheels, shoot long and lovely
        and lush;
    Thrush's eggs look little low heavens, and thrush
Through the echoing timber does so rinse and wring
The ear, it strikes like lightnings to hear him sing;
    The glassy peartree leaves and blooms, they brush
    The descending blue; that blue is all in a rush
With richness; the racing lambs too have fair their fling.

What is all this juice and all this joy?
    A strain of the earth's sweet being in the beginning
In Eden garden. – Have, get, before it cloy,

    Before it cloud, Christ, lord, and sour with sinning,
Innocent mind and Mayday in girl and boy,
    Most, O maid's child, thy choice and worthy
        the winning.

GERARD MANLEY HOPKINS

BLACK MARCH

I have a friend
At the end
Of the world.
His name is a breath

Of fresh air.
He is dressed in
Grey chiffon. At least
I think it is chiffon.
It has a
Peculiar look, like smoke.

It wraps him round
It blows out of place
It conceals him
I have not seen his face.

But I have seen his eyes, they are
As pretty and bright
As raindrops on black twigs
In March, and heard him say:

I am a breath
Of fresh air for you, a change
By and by.

Black March I call him
Because of his eyes
Being like March raindrops
On black twigs.

(Such a pretty time when the sky
Behind black twigs can be seen
Stretched out in one
Uninterrupted
Cambridge blue as cold as snow.)

But this friend
Whatever new names I give him
Is an old friend. He says:

Whatever names you give me
I am
A breath of fresh air,
A change for you.

STEVIE SMITH   33

SPRING POOLS

These pools that, though in forests, still reflect
The total sky almost without defect,
And like the flowers beside them, chill and shiver,
Will like the flowers beside them soon be gone,
And yet not out by any brook or river,
But up by roots to bring dark foliage on.

The trees that have it in their pent-up buds
To darken nature and be summer woods –
Let them think twice before they use their powers
To blot out and drink up and sweep away
These flowery waters and these watery flowers
From snow that melted only yesterday.

"LOVELIEST OF TREES"

Loveliest of trees, the cherry now
Is hung with bloom along the bough,
And stands about the woodland ride
Wearing white for Eastertide.

Now, of my threescore years and ten,
Twenty will not come again,
And take from seventy springs a score,
It only leaves me fifty more.

And since to look at things in bloom
Fifty springs are little room,
About the woodlands I will go
To see the cherry hung with snow.

A. E. HOUSMAN

MARCH MORNING UNLIKE OTHERS

Blue haze. Bees hanging in air at the hive-mouth.
Crawling in prone stupor of sun
On the hive-lip. Snowdrops. Two buzzards,
Still-wings, each
Magnetised to the other,
Float orbits.
Cattle standing warm. Lit, happy stillness.
A raven, under the hill,
Coughing among bare oaks.
Aircraft, elated, splitting blue.
Leisure to stand. The knee-deep mud at the trough
Stiffening. Lambs freed to be foolish.

The earth invalid, dropsied, bruised, wheeled
Out into the sun,
After the frightful operation.
She lies back, wounds undressed to the sun,
To be healed,
Sheltered from the sneapy chill creeping North wind,
Leans back, eyes closed, exhausted, smiling
Into the sun. Perhaps dozing a little.
While we sit, and smile, and wait, and know
She is not going to die.

PUTTING IN THE SEED

You come to fetch me from my work tonight
When supper's on the table, and we'll see
If I can leave off burying the white
Soft petals fallen from the apple tree
(Soft petals, yes, but not so barren quite,
Mingled with these, smooth bean and wrinkled pea;)
And go along with you ere you lose sight
Of what you came for and become like me,
Slave to a springtime passion for the earth.
How Love burns through the Putting in the Seed
On through the watching for that early birth
When, just as the soil tarnishes with weed,
The sturdy seedling with arched body comes
Shouldering its way and shedding the earth crumbs.

SPRING

When daisies pied and violets blue,
    And lady-smocks all silver-white,
And cuckoo-buds of yellow hue
    Do paint the meadows with delight,
The cuckoo then, on every tree,
Mocks married men, for thus sings he,
      Cuckoo, cuckoo! O word of fear,
      Unpleasing to a married ear.

When shepherds pipe on oaten straws,
    And merry larks are ploughmen's clocks,
When turtles tread, and rooks, and daws,
    And maidens bleach their summer smocks,
The cuckoo then, on every tree,
Mocks married men, for thus sings he,
      Cuckoo, cuckoo! O word of fear,
      Unpleasing to a married ear.

THE LENT LILY

'Tis spring; come out to ramble
    The hilly brakes around,
For under thorn and bramble
    About the hollow ground
    The primroses are found.

And there's the windflower chilly
    With all the winds at play,
And there's the Lenten lily
    That has not long to stay
    And dies on Easter day.

And since till girls go maying
    You find the primrose still,
And find the windflower playing
    With every wind at will,
    But not the daffodil,

Bring baskets now, and sally
    Upon the spring's array,
And bear from hill and valley
    The daffodil away
    That dies on Easter day.

A. E. HOUSMAN

SPRING SONG II

And now my spring beauties,
Things of the earth,
Beetles, shards and wings of moth
And snail houses left
From last summer's wreck,
Now spring smoke
Of the burned dead leaves
And veils of the scent
Of some secret plant,

Come, my beauties, teach me,
Let me have your wild surprise,
Yes, and tell me on my knees
Of your new life.

ANOTHER APRIL

The panes flash, tremble with your ghostly passage
Through them, an x-ray sheerness billowing,
    and I have risen
But cannot speak, remembering only that one was meant
To rise and not to speak. Young storm, this house is
    yours.
Let your eye darken, your rain come, the candle reeling
Deep in what still reflects control itself and me.
Daybreak's great gray rust-veined irises humble
    and proud
Along your path will have laid their foreheads in
    the dust.

RESURRECTIONS

In spring
a bluster
busting up

against a
wall will
lift last

year's leaves
higher than
trees did.

A COLD SPRING
For Jane Dewey, Maryland

Nothing is so beautiful as spring – HOPKINS

A cold spring:
the violet was flawed on the lawn.
For two weeks or more the trees hesitated;
the little leaves waited,
carefully indicating their characteristics.
Finally a grave green dust
settled over your big and aimless hills.
One day, in a chill white blast of sunshine,
on the side of one a calf was born.
The mother stopped lowing
and took a long time eating the after-birth,
a wretched flag,
but the calf got up promptly
and seemed inclined to feel gay.

The next day
was much warmer.
Greenish-white dogwood infiltrated the wood,
each petal burned, apparently, by a cigarette-butt;
and the blurred redbud stood
beside it, motionless, but almost more
like movement than any placeable color.
Four deer practised leaping over your fences.

The infant oak-leaves swung through the sober oak.
Song-sparrows were wound up for the summer,
and in the maple the complementary cardinal
cracked a whip, and the sleeper awoke,
stretching miles of green limbs from the south.
In his cap the lilacs whitened,
then one day they fell like snow.
Now, in the evening,
a new moon comes.
The hills grow softer. Tufts of long grass show
where each cow-flop lies.
The bull-frogs are sounding,
slack strings plucked by heavy thumbs.
Beneath the light, against your white front door,
the smallest moths, like Chinese fans,
flatten themselves, silver and silver-gilt
over pale yellow, orange, or gray.
Now, from the thick grass, the fireflies
begin to rise:
up, then down, then up again:
lit on the ascending flight,
drifting simultaneously to the same height,
– exactly like the bubbles in champagne.
– Later on they rise much higher.
And your shadowy pastures will be able to offer
these particular glowing tributes
every evening now throughout the summer.

LINES WRITTEN IN EARLY SPRING

I heard a thousand blended notes,
While in a grove I sate reclined,
In that sweet mood when pleasant thoughts
Bring sad thoughts to the mind.

To her fair works did Nature link
The human soul that through me ran;
And much it grieved my heart to think
What man has made of man.

Through primrose tufts, in that green bower,
The periwinkle trailed its wreaths;
And 'tis my faith that every flower
Enjoys the air it breathes.

The birds around me hopped and played,
Their thoughts I cannot measure: –
But the least motion which they made,
It seemed a thrill of pleasure.

The budding twigs spread out their fan,
To catch the breezy air;
And I must think, do all I can,
That there was pleasure there.

If this belief from heaven be sent,
If such be Nature's holy plan,
Have I not reason to lament
What man has made of man?

SONNET TO SPRING

The brown, unpleasant,
aggressively ribbed and
unpliant leaves of the loquat,
shaped like bark canoes that
something squashed flat,
litter the spring cement.
A fat-cheeked whim of air –
a French *vent* or some similar affair –
with enough choices in the front yard
for a blossomy puff worthy of Fragonard,
instead expends its single breath
beneath one leathery leaf of loquat
which flops over and again lies flat.
Spring is frivolous like that.

SPRING

Spring, the sweet spring, is the year's pleasant king;
Then blooms each thing, then maids dance in a ring,
Cold doth not sting, the pretty birds do sing:
    Cuckoo, jug-jug, pu-we, to-witta-woo!

The palm and may make country houses gay,
Lambs frisk and play, the shepherds pipe all day,
And we hear aye birds tune this merry lay:
    Cuckoo, jug-jug, pu-we, to-witta-woo!

The fields breathe sweet, the daisies kiss our feet,
Young lovers meet, old wives a-sunning sit,
In every street these tunes our ears do greet:
    Cuckoo, jug-jug, pu-we, to-witta-woo!
        Spring, the sweet spring!

CORINNA'S GOING A-MAYING

Get up, get up for shame, the blooming morn
Upon her wings presents the god unshorn.
    See how Aurora throws her fair
    Fresh-quilted colours through the air:
    Get up, sweet slug-a-bed, and see
    The dew bespangling herb and tree.
Each flower has wept, and bowèd toward the east,
Above an hour since; yet you not drest,
    Nay! not so much as out of bed?
    When all the birds have matins said,
    And sung their thankful hymns, 'tis sin,
    Nay, profanation to keep in,
Whenas a thousand virgins on this day
Spring sooner than the lark to fetch in May.

Rise and put on your foliage, and be seen
To come forth, like the spring-time, fresh and green,
    And sweet as Flora. Take no care
    For jewels for your gown or hair:
    Fear not; the leaves will strew
    Gems in abundance upon you:
Besides, the childhood of the day has kept,
Against you come, some orient pearls unwept.
    Come, and receive them while the light
    Hangs on the dew-locks of the night,

And Titan on the eastern hill
　　Retires himself, or else stands still
Till you come forth. Wash, dress, be brief in praying:
Few beads are best when once we go a-Maying.

Come, my Corinna, come; and coming, mark
How each field turns a street, each street a park
　　Made green and trimmed with trees: see how
　　Devotion gives each house a bough
　　Or branch; each porch, each door, ere this,
　　An ark, a tabernacle is,
Made up of white-thorn neatly interwove,
As if here were those cooler shades of love.
　　Can such delights be in the street
　　And open fields, and we not see't?
　　Come, we'll abroad: and let's obey
　　The proclamation made for May,
And sin no more, as we have done, by staying;
But, my Corinna, come, let's go a-Maying.

There's not a budding boy or girl this day
But is got up and gone to bring in May.
　　A deal of youth, ere this, is come
　　Back and with white-thorn laden home.
　　Some have dispatched their cakes and cream,
　　Before that we have left to dream:

And some have wept and wooed, and plighted troth,
And chose their priest, ere we can cast off sloth:
    Many a green-gown has been given;
    Many a kiss, both odd and even;
    Many a glance too has been sent
    From out the eye, love's firmament:
Many a jest told of the keys betraying
This night, and locks picked: yet we're not a-Maying.

Come, let us go, while we are in our prime,
And take the harmless folly of the time.
    We shall grow old apace, and die
    Before we know our liberty.
    Our life is short, and our days run
    As fast away as does the sun.
And as a vapour or a drop of rain,
Once lost, can ne'er be found again:
    So when or you or I are made
    A fable, song, or fleeting shade,
    All love, all liking, all delight
    Lies drowned with us in endless night.
Then, while time serves, and we are but decaying,
Come, my Corinna, come, let's go a-Maying.

THE WIDOW'S LAMENT
IN SPRINGTIME

Sorrow is my own yard
where the new grass
flames as it has flamed
often before but not
with the cold fire
that closes round me this year.
Thirtyfive years
I lived with my husband.
The plumtree is white today
with masses of flowers.
Masses of flowers
load the cherry branches
and color some bushes
yellow and some red
but the grief in my heart
is stronger than they
for though they were my joy
formerly, today I notice them
and turn away forgetting.
Today my son told me
that in the meadows,
at the edge of the heavy woods
in the distance, he saw
trees of white flowers.

I feel that I would like
to go there
and fall into those flowers
and sink into the marsh near them.

THE ENKINDLED SPRING

This spring as it comes bursts up in bonfires green,
Wild puffing of green-fire trees, and flame-green
    bushes,
Thorn-blossom lifting in wreaths of smoke between
Where the wood fumes up, and the flickering,
    watery rushes.

I am amazed at this spring, this conflagration
Of green fires lit on the soil of earth, this blaze
Of growing, these smoke-puffs that puff in wild
    gyration,
Faces of people blowing across my gaze!

And I, what sort of fire am I among
This conflagration of spring? the gap in it all –!
Not even palish smoke like the rest of the throng.
Less than the wind that runs to the flamy call!

"I SO LIKED SPRING"

I so liked Spring last year
    Because you were here; –
        The thrushes too –
Because it was these you so liked to hear –
      I so liked you.

    This year's a different thing, –
      I'll not think of you.
But I'll like Spring because it is simply Spring
      As the thrushes do.

"A LITTLE MADNESS IN THE SPRING"

A little Madness in the Spring
Is wholesome even for the King,
But God be with the Clown —

Who ponders this tremendous scene —
This whole Experiment of Green —
As if it were his own!

ANOTHER SPRING

If I might see another Spring,
    I'd not plant summer flowers and wait:
I'd have my crocuses at once,
My leafless pink mezereons,
    My chill-veined snowdrops, choicer yet
    My white or azure-violet,
Leaf-nested primrose; anything
    To blow at once, not late.

If I might see another Spring,
    I'd listen to the daylight birds
That build their nests and pair and sing,
Nor wait for mateless nightingale;
    I'd listen to the lusty herds,
    The ewes with lambs as white as snow,
I'd find out music in the hail
    And all the winds that blow.

If I might see another Spring –
    Oh stinging comment on my past
That all my past results in "if" –
    If I might see another Spring,
I'd laugh to-day, to-day is brief;
I would not wait for anything:
    I'd use to-day that cannot last,
    Be glad to-day and sing.

NAMING OF PARTS

Today we have naming of parts. Yesterday,
We had daily cleaning. And tomorrow morning,
We shall have what to do after firing. But today,
Today we have naming of parts. Japonica
Glistens like coral in all of the neighboring gardens,
   And today we have naming of parts.

This is the lower sling swivel. And this
Is the upper sling swivel, whose use you will see,
When you are given your slings. And this is the piling
    swivel,
Which in your case you have not got. The branches
Hold in the gardens their silent, eloquent gestures,
   Which in our case we have not got.

This is the safety-catch, which is always released
With an easy flick of the thumb. And please do not
    let me
See anyone using his finger. You can do it quite easy
If you have any strength in your thumb. The blossoms
Are fragile and motionless, never letting anyone see
   Any of them using their finger.

And this you can see is the bolt. The purpose of this
Is to open the breech, as you see. We can slide it

Rapidly backwards and forwards: we call this
Easing the spring. And rapidly backwards and forwards
   The early bees are assaulting and fumbling the flowers:
      They call it easing the Spring.

They call it easing the Spring: it is perfectly easy
If you have any strength in your thumb: like the bolt,
And the breech, and the cocking-piece, and the point
   of balance,
Which in our case we have not got; and the almond-
   blossom
Silent in all of the gardens and the bees going backwards
   and forwards,
   For today we have naming of parts.

APRIL LIGHT

Lined with light
the twigs are stubby arrows.
A gilded trunk writhes
upward from the roots,
from the pit of the black tentacles.

In the book of spring
a bare-limbed torso
is the first illustration.

Light teaches the tree
to beget leaves,
to embroider itself all over
with green reality,
until summer becomes
its steady portrait,
and birds bring their lifetime
to the boughs.

Then even the corpse
light copies from below
may shimmer, dreaming it feels
the cheeks of blossom.

A STORM IN APRIL
For Ben

Some winters, taking leave,
Deal us a last, hard blow,
Salting the ground like Carthage
Before they will go.

But the bright, milling snow
Which throngs the air today –
It is a way of leaving
So as to stay.

The light flakes do not weigh
The willows down, but sift
Through the white catkins, loose
As petal-drift,

Or in an up-draft lift
And glitter at a height,
Dazzling as summer's leaf-stir
Chinked with light.

This storm, if I am right,
Will not be wholly over
Till green fields, here and there,
Turn white with clover,

And through chill air the puffs of milkweed hover.

RICHARD WILBUR 61

TO DAFFODILS

Fair daffodils, we weep to see
    You haste away so soon:
As yet the early-rising sun
    Has not attained his noon.
            Stay, stay,
        Until the hasting day
            Has run
        But to the evensong;
And, having prayed together, we
    Will go with you along.

We have short time to stay, as you,
    We have as short a spring;
As quick a growth to meet decay,
    As you, or anything.
            We die,
        As your hours do, and dry
            Away,
        Like to the summer's rain;
Or as the pearls of morning's dew
    Ne'er to be found again.

THERE WILL COME SOFT RAINS
(War Time)

There will come soft rains and the smell of the ground,
And swallows circling with their shimmering sound;

And frogs in the pools singing at night,
And wild plum-trees in tremulous white;

Robins will wear their feathery fire
Whistling their whims on a low fence-wire;

And not one will know of the war, not one
Will care at last when it is done.

Not one would mind, neither bird nor tree
If mankind perished utterly;

And Spring herself, when she woke at dawn,
Would scarcely know that we were gone.

SARA TEASDALE

HOME-THOUGHTS, FROM ABROAD

Oh, to be in England
Now that April's there,
And whoever wakes in England
Sees, some morning, unaware,
That the lowest boughs and the brushwood sheaf
Round the elm-tree bole are in tiny leaf,
While the chaffinch sings on the orchard bough
In England – now!

And after April, when May follows,
And the whitethroat builds, and all the swallows!
Hark, where my blossomed pear-tree in the hedge
Leans to the field and scatters on the clover
Blossoms and dewdrops – at the bent spray's edge –
That's the wise thrush; he sings each song twice over,
Lest you should think he never could recapture
The first fine careless rapture!
And though the fields look rough with hoary dew,
All will be gay when noontide wakes anew
The buttercups, the little children's dower
– Far brighter than this gaudy melon-flower!

APRIL IN TOWN

Straight from the east the wind blows sharp with rain,
  That just now drove its wild ranks down the street,
  And westward rushed into the sunset sweet.
Spouts brawl, boughs drip and cease and drip again,
Bricks gleam; keen saffron glows each window-pane,
  And every pool beneath the passing feet.
  Innumerable odors fine and fleet
Are blown this way from blossoming lawn and lane.
Wet roofs show black against a tender sky;
  The almond bushes in the lean-fenced square,
    Beaten to the walks, show all their draggled white.
A troop of laborers comes slowly by;
  One bears a daffodil, and seems to bear
    A new-lit candle through the fading light.

[IN JUST-]

in Just-
spring   when the world is mud-
luscious the little
lame balloonman

whistles   fat   and wee

andrunning from marbles and
piracies and it's
spring

when the world is puddle-wonderful

the queer
old balloonman
fat   and   wee
and bettyandisbel come dancing

from hop-scotch and jump-rope and

it's
spring
and
    the

goat-footed

    balloonMan   whistles

    far

    and

    wee

OUT OF MAY'S SHOWS SELECTED

Apple orchards, the trees all cover'd with blossoms;
Wheat fields carpeted far and near in vital
    emerald green;
The eternal, exhaustless freshness of each
    early morning;
The yellow, golden, transparent haze of the warm
    afternoon sun;
The aspiring lilac bushes with profuse purple or
    white flowers.

SPRING

Somewhere
    a black bear
        has just risen from sleep
            and is staring

down the mountain.
    All night
        in the brisk and shallow restlessness
            of early spring

I think of her,
    her four black fists
        flicking the gravel,
            her tongue

like a red fire
    touching the grass,
        the cold water.
            There is only one question:

how to love this world.
    I think of her
        rising
            like a black and leafy ledge

to sharpen her claws against
    the silence
        of the trees.
            Whatever else

my life is
    with its poems
        and its music
            and its glass cities,

it is also this dazzling darkness
    coming
        down the mountain,
            breathing and tasting;

all day I think of her —
    her white teeth,
        her wordlessness,
            her perfect love.

SUMMER

"SUMMER IS Y-COMEN IN"

Summer is y-comen in,
Loud sing cuckoo!
Groweth seed and bloweth meed
And springeth the wood now –
Sing cuckoo!
Ewe bleateth after lamb,
Loweth after calf cow;
Bullock starteth, buck farteth.
Merry sing cuckoo!
Cuckoo! Cuckoo!
Well singest thou cuckoo:
Nor cease thou never now.
     Sing cuckoo, now, sing cuckoo!
     Sing cuckoo! sing cuckoo, now!

ANON.

ROUNDEL

Now welcome, summer, with thy sunnė soft,
That hast this winter's wedres overshake
And driven away the longė nightės black!

Saint Valentine, that art full high aloft,
Thus singen smallė fowlės for thy sake:
  "Now welcome, summer, with thy sunnė soft,
  That hast this winter's wedres overshake!"

Well have they causė for to gladden oft,
Since each of them recovered hath his make;
Full blissful may they singė when they wake:
  "Now welcome, summer, with thy sunnė soft,
  That hast this winter's wedres overshake
    And driven away the longė nightės black!"

THE HOUSE WAS QUIET AND THE WORLD WAS CALM

The house was quiet and the world was calm.
The reader became the book; and summer night

Was like the conscious being of the book.
The house was quiet and the world was calm.

The words were spoken as if there was no book,
Except that the reader leaned above the page,

Wanted to lean, wanted much most to be
The scholar to whom his book is true, to whom

The summer night is like a perfection of thought.
The house was quiet because it had to be.

The quiet was part of the meaning, part of the mind:
The access of perfection to the page.

And the world was calm. The truth in a calm world,
In which there is no other meaning, itself

Is calm, itself is summer and night, itself
Is the reader leaning late and reading there.

WALLACE STEVENS   75

"FURTHER IN SUMMER
THAN THE BIRDS"

Further in Summer than the Birds
Pathetic from the Grass
A minor Nation celebrates
Its unobtrusive Mass.

No Ordinance be seen
So gradual the Grace
A pensive Custom it becomes
Enlarging Loneliness.

Antiquest felt at Noon
When August burning low
Arise this spectral Canticle
Repose to typify

Remit as yet no Grace
No Furrow on the Glow
Yet a Druidic Difference
Enhances Nature now

THE SWEET SEASON

The sweet season, that bud and bloom forth brings
With green hath clad the hill, and eke the vale;
The nightingale with feathers new she sings;
The turtle to her make hath told her tale.
Summer is come, for every spray now springs;
The hart hath hung his old head on the pale;
The buck in brake his winter coat he flings;
The fishes float with new-repairèd scale;
The adder all her slough aways she slings;
The swift swallow pursueth the flies small;
The busy bee her honey now she mings
Winter is worn that was the flowers' bale.
    And thus I see among these pleasant things
    Which care decays, and yet my sorrow springs.

AT THE ROYAL ACADEMY

These summer landscapes – clump, and copse,
    and croft –
Woodland and meadowland – here hung aloft,
Gay with limp grass and leafery new and soft,

Seem caught from the immediate season's yield
I saw last noonday shining over the field,
By rapid snatch, while still are uncongealed

The saps that in their live originals climb;
Yester's quick greenage here set forth in mime
Just as it stands, now, at our breathing-time.

But these young foils so fresh upon each tree,
Soft verdures spread in sprouting novelty,
Are not this summer's though they feign to be.

Last year their May to Michaelmas term was run,
Last autumn browned and buried every one,
And no more know they sight of any sun.

"WOOF OF THE SUN"

Woof of the sun, ethereal gauze,
Woven of Nature's richest stuffs,
Visible heat, air-water, and dry sea,
Last conquest of the eye;
Toil of the day displayed, sun-dust,
Aerial surf upon the shores of earth,
Ethereal estuary, frith of light,
Breakers of air, billows of heat,
Fine summer spray on inland seas;
Bird of the sun, transparent-winged
Owlet of noon, soft-pinioned,
From heath or stubble rising without song;
Establish thy serenity o'er the fields.

SUMMER POEM

Leaving the house,
I went out to see

the frog, for example,
in her shining green skin;

and her eggs
like a slippery veil;

and her eyes
with their golden rims;

and the pond
with its risen lilies;

and its warmed shores
dotted with pink flowers;

and the long, windless afternoon;
and the white heron

like a dropped cloud,
taking one slow step

then standing awhile then taking
another, writing

her own soft-footed poem
through the still waters.

END OF MAY

Atop each stem
an iris or two has turned in
on itself with no regrets and given up
color. Pink, yellow and red,
the rosepetals are spread
so wide they already tend
toward total drop.
Peony litter covers the ground.
On earlier days
friends and neighbors in pairs have been summoned
to have a drink and see the bloom,
have admired everything and gone.

I sit in my suntan oil alone –
almost alone – a jay
tries to flap me away
from his drinking trough.
His coarse, demanding rebukes
pierce my ears. He chirks
news of impending drouth.

But under my feet as I tan
is no longer a brick patio,
rather a light brown
paisley made of seed wings

from the silver maple, which can sow
faster than I can sew
this fine fabric into something.
And in the air,
like a great snow,
are flakes alive with purpose.
The cottonwood huffs and puffs
them everywhere.

On oil that sheathes me from sun
they cling to bare parts of person.
All the long, late
day, my arms and legs are furred
with such a will to beget
I think I can almost afford
to forget it's only skin-deep.
It's like taking dope.

It's too late, I tell the tree,
you've settled on somebody seedless.
Equivocally, it nods its head.
But I have been overheard.
Maybe for you but not for me,
the seedy old world says.

I THINK

I will write you a letter,
June day. Dear June Fifth,
you're all in green, so
many kinds and all one
green, tree shadows on
grass blades and grass
blade shadows. The air
fills up with motor
mower sound. The cat
walks up the drive
a dead baby rabbit
in her maw. The sun
is hot, the breeze
is cool. And suddenly
in all the green
the lilacs bloom,
massive and exquisite
in color and shape
and scent. The roses
are more full of
buds than ever. No
flowers. But soon.
June day, you have
your own perfection:

so green to say
goodbye to. Green,
stick around
a while.

SUMMER MOODS

I love at eventide to walk alone
Down narrow lanes o'erhung with dewy thorn
Where from the long grass underneath the snail
Jet black creeps out and sprouts his timid horn.
I love to muse o'er meadows newly mown
Where withering grass perfumes the sultry air
Where bees search round with sad and weary drone
In vain for flowers that bloomed but newly there,
While in the juicy corn the hidden quail
Cries "wet my foot" and hid as thoughts unborn
The fairy-like and seldom-seen land rail
Utters "craik craik" like voices underground
Right glad to meet the evening's dewy veil
And see the light fade into glooms around.

JOHN CLARE   85

ON THE GRASSHOPPER AND
THE CRICKET

The poetry of earth is never dead:
    When all the birds are faint with the hot sun,
    And hide in cooling trees, a voice will run
From hedge to hedge about the new-mown mead;
That is the Grasshopper's – he takes the lead
    In summer luxury, – he has never done
    With his delights; for when tired out with fun
He rests at ease beneath some pleasant weed.
The poetry of earth is ceasing never:
    On a lone winter evening, when the frost
      Has wrought a silence, from the stove there shrills
The Cricket's song, in warmth increasing ever,
    And seems to one in drowsiness half lost,
      The Grasshopper's among some grassy hills.

PEAR TREE

Silver dust,
lifted from the earth,
higher than my arms reach,
you have mounted,
O, silver,
higher than my arms reach,
you front us with great mass;

no flower ever opened
so staunch a white leaf,
no flower ever parted silver
from such rare silver;

O, white pear,
your flower-tufts
thick on the branch
bring summer and ripe fruits
in their purple hearts.

SUMMER NIGHT

The sounds
Of the Harlem night
Drop one by one into stillness.
The last player-piano is closed.
The last victrola ceases with the
"Jazz Boy Blues."
The last crying baby sleeps
And the night becomes
Still as a whispering heartbeat.
I toss
Without rest in the darkness,
Weary as the tired night,
My soul
Empty as the silence,
Empty with a vague,
Aching emptiness,
Desiring,
Needing someone,
Something.
I toss without rest
In the darkness
Until the new dawn,
Wan and pale,
Descends like a white mist
Into the court-yard.

JUNE IN THE SUBURBS

Not with a whimper but a roar
Of birth and bloom this month commences.
The wren's a gossip at her door.
Roses explode along the fences.

By day the chattering mowers cope
With grass decreed a final winner.
Darkness delays. The skipping rope
Twirls in the driveway after dinner.

Through lupine-lighted borders now
For winter bones Dalmatians forage.
Costly, the spray on apple bough.
The canvas chair comes out of storage;

And rose-red golfers dream of par,
And class-bound children loathe their labors,
While pilgrims, touring gardens, are
Cold to petunias of their neighbors.

Now from damp loafers nightly spills
The sand. Brides lodge their lists with Plummer.
And cooks devise on charcoal grills
The first burnt offerings of summer.

PHYLLIS McGINLEY

TREES

To be a giant and keep quiet about it,
To stay in one's own place;
To stand for the constant presence of process
And always to seem the same;
To be steady as a rock and always trembling,
Having the hard appearance of death
With the soft, fluent nature of growth,
One's Being deceptively armored,
One's Becoming deceptively vulnerable;
To be so tough, and take the light so well,
Freely providing forbidden knowledge
Of so many things about heaven and earth
For which we should otherwise have no word –
Poems or people are rarely so lovely,
And even when they have great qualities
They tend to tell you rather than exemplify
What they believe themselves to be about,
While from the moving silence of trees,
Whether in storm or calm, in leaf and naked,
Night or day, we draw conclusions of our own,
Sustaining and unnoticed as our breath,
And perilous also – though there has never been
A critical tree – about the nature of things.

LINDENBLOOM

Before midsummer density
opaques with shade the checker-
tables underneath, in daylight
unleafing lindens burn
green-gold a day or two,
no more, with intimations
of an essence I saw once,
in what had been the pleasure-
garden of the popes
at Avignon, dishevel

into half (or possibly three-
quarters of) a million
hanging, intricately
tactile, blond bell-pulls
of bloom, the in-mid-air
resort of honeybees'
hirsute cotillion
teasing by the milligram
out of those necklaced
nectaries, aromas

so intensely subtle,
strollers passing under
looked up confused,

as though they'd just
heard voices, or
inhaled the ghost
of derelict splendor
and/or of seraphs shaken
into pollen dust
no transubstantiating
pope or antipope could sift
or quite precisely ponder.

HEAT

O wind, rend open the heat,
cut apart the heat,
rend it to tatters.

Fruit cannot drop
through this thick air –
fruit cannot fall into heat
that presses up and blunts
the points of pears
and rounds the grapes.

Cut the heat –
plough through it,
turning it on either side
of your path.

H.D.

A JULY AFTERNOON BY THE POND

The fervent heat, but so much more endurable in this
pure air – the white and pink pond-blossoms, with
great heart-shaped leaves; the glassy waters of the
creek, the banks, with dense bushery, and the
picturesque beeches and shade and turf; the tremulous,
reedy call of some bird from recesses, breaking the
warm, indolent, half-voluptuous silence; an occasional
wasp, hornet, honey-bee or bumble (they hover near
my hands or face, yet annoy me not, nor I them, as
they appear to examine, find nothing, and away they
go) – the vast space of the sky overhead so clear, and
the buzzard up there sailing his slow whirl in majestic
spirals and discs; just over the surface of the pond,
two large slate-color'd dragon-flies, with wings of
lace, circling and darting and occasionally balancing
themselves quite still, their wings quivering all the
time, (are they not showing off for my amusement?) –
the pond itself, with the sword-shaped calamus; the
water snakes – occasionally a flitting blackbird, with
red dabs on his shoulders, as he darts slantingly by –
the sounds that bring out the solitude, warmth, light
and shade – the quawk of some pond duck – (the
crickets and grasshoppers are mute in the noon heat,
but I hear the song of the first cicadas;) – then at
some distance the rattle and whirr of a reaping

machine as the horses draw it on a rapid walk
through a rye field on the opposite side of the creek –
(what was the yellow or light-brown bird, large as a
young hen, with short neck and long-stretch'd legs
I just saw, in flapping and awkward flight over there
through the trees?) – the prevailing delicate, yet
palpable, spicy, grassy, clovery perfume to my
nostrils; and over all, encircling all, to my sight and
soul, the free space of the sky, transparent and blue –
and hovering there in the west, a mass of white-gray
fleecy clouds the sailors call "shoals of mackerel" –
the sky, with silver swirls like locks of toss'd hair,
spreading, expanding – a vast voiceless, formless
simulacrum – yet may-be the most real reality and
formulator of everything – who knows?

WALT WHITMAN

MIDSUMMER

This starbreak is celestial air
Just silver; earthlight, dying amber.
Underneath an arch of pallor
Summer keeps her brightened chamber.

Bright beauty of the risen dust
And deep flood-mark of beauty pressed
Up from earth in lovely flower,
High against my lonely breast;

Only before the waters fall
Is Paradise shore for gaining now.
The grasses drink the berry-bright dew;
The small fruits jewel all the bough.

Heartbreaking summer beyond taste,
Ripeness and frost are soon to know;
But might such color hold the west,
And time, and time, be honey-slow!

SUMMER SONG
(Eskimo)

Aya!
Ayaya, it is beautiful, beautiful it is out-doors when
    the summer comes at last.
Ayaya, ayaya, aya!

Ayaya, it is beautiful, beautiful it is out-doors when
    the reindeer begin to come,
Ayaya, ayaya, aya!

Ayaya, when the roaring river rushes from the hills
    in summer.
Ayaya, ayaya, aya!

Ayaya, there is no reason for me to be mournful when
    the gulls cease crying.
Ayaya, ayaya, aya!

Ayaya, plenty of meat I shall have and plenty codfish.
Ayaya, ayaya, aya!

Ayaya, it is beautiful, beautiful it is out-doors when
    the summer comes at last.
Ayaya, ayaya, aya!

ANON., TRANS. FRANZ BOAS

HEATWAVE

Between Westminster and sunstruck St Paul's
The desert has entered the flea's belly.

Like shut-eyed, half-submerged Nile bulls
The buildings tremble with breath.

The mirage of river is so real
Bodies drift in it, and human rubbish.

The main thing is the silence.
There are no charts for the silence.

Men can't penetrate it. Till sundown
Releases its leopard

Over the roofs, and women are suddenly
Everywhere, and the walker's bones

Melt in the coughing of great cats.

FLAG OF SUMMER

Sky and sea and sand,
fabric of the day.
The eye compares each band.

Parallels of color on bare
canvas of time-by-the-sea.
Linen-clean the air.

Tan of the burlap
beach scuffed with prints
of bathers. Green and dapple,

the serpentine swipe
of the sea unraveling
a ragged crepe

on the shore. Heavy satin
far out, the coil,
darkening, flattens

to the sky's rim.
There a gauze screen,
saturate-blue, shimmers.

Blue and green and tan,
the fabric changes hues
by brush of light or rain:

sky's violet bar
leans over flinty waves
opaque as the shore's

opaline grains; sea silvers,
clouds fade to platinum,
the sand-mat ripples

with greenish tints
of snakeskin, or drying,
whitens to tent-cloth

spread in the sun. These bands,
primary in their dimensions,
elements, textures, strands:

the flag of summer,
emblem of ease, triple-striped,
each day salutes the swimmer.

SUMMER WIND

It is a sultry day; the sun has drank
The dew that lay upon the morning grass,
There is no rustling in the lofty elm
That canopies my dwelling, and its shade
Scarce cools me. All is silent, save the faint
And interrupted murmur of the bee,
Settling on the sick flowers, and then again
Instantly on the wing. The plants around
Feel the too potent fervors; the tall maize
Rolls up its long green leaves; the clover droops
Its tender foliage, and declines its blooms.
But far in the fierce sunshine tower the hills,
With all their growth of woods, silent and stern,
As if the scorching heat and dazzling light
Were but an element they loved. Bright clouds,
Motionless pillars of the brazen heaven; —
Their bases on the mountains — their white tops
Shining in the far ether — fire the air
With a reflected radiance, and make turn
The gazer's eye away. For me, I lie
Languidly in the shade, where the thick turf,
Yet virgin from the kisses of the sun,
Retains some freshness, and I woo the wind
That still delays its coming. Why so slow,
Gentle and voluble spirit of the air?

Oh, come and breathe upon the fainting earth
Coolness and life. Is it that in his caves
He hears me? See, on yonder woody ridge,
The pine is bending his proud top, and now,
Among the nearer groves, chestnut and oak
Are tossing their green boughs about. He comes!
Lo, where the grassy meadow runs in waves!
The deep distressful silence of the scene
Breaks up with mingling of unnumbered sounds
And universal motion. He is come,
Shaking a shower of blossoms from the shrubs,
And bearing on their fragrance; and he brings
Music of birds, and rustling of young boughs,
And sound of swaying branches, and the voice
Of distant waterfalls. All the green herbs
Are stirring in his breath; a thousand flowers,
By the road-side and the borders of the brook,
Nod gaily to each other; glossy leaves
Are twinkling in the sun, as if the dew
Were on them yet, and silver waters break
Into small waves and sparkle as he comes.

THE SUMMER RAIN

My books I'd fain cast off, I cannot read,
'Twixt every page my thoughts go stray at large
Down in the meadow, where is richer feed,
And will not mind to hit their proper targe.

Plutarch was good, and so was Homer too,
Our Shakespeare's life was rich to live again,
What Plutarch read that was not good nor true,
Nor Shakespeare's books, unless his books were men.

Here while I lie beneath this walnut bough,
What care I for the Greeks, or for Troy town,
If juster battles are enacted now
Between the ants upon this hummock's crown.

Bid Homer wait till I the issue learn,
If red or black the gods will favor most,
Or yonder Ajax will the phalanx turn,
Struggling to heave some rock against the host.

Tell Shakespeare to attend some leisure hour,
For now I've business with this drop of dew,
And see you not, the clouds prepare a shower, –
I'll meet him shortly when the sky is blue.

This bed of herdsgrass and wild oats was spread
Last year with nicer skill than monarchs use,
A clover tuft is pillow for my head,
And violets quite overtop my shoes.

And now the cordial clouds have shut all in,
And gently swells the wind to say all's well,
The scattered drops are falling fast and thin,
Some in the pond, some in the lily bell.

Drip, drip the trees for all the country round,
And richness rare distils from every bough,
The wind alone it is makes every sound,
Shaking down crystals on the leaves below.

For shame the sun will never show himself,
Who could not with his beams e'er melt me so,
My dripping locks – they would become an elf
Who in a beaded coat does gaily go.

THE RAINY SUMMER

There's much afoot in heaven and earth this year;
  The winds hunt up the sun, hunt up the moon,
Trouble the dubious dawn, hasten the drear
  Height of a threatening noon.

No breath of boughs, no breath of leaves, of fronds,
  May linger or grow warm; the trees are loud;
The forest, rooted, tosses in her bonds,
  And strains against the cloud.

No scents may pause within the garden-fold;
  The rifled flowers are cold as ocean-shells;
Bees, humming in the storm, carry their cold
  Wild honey to cold cells.

MY FATHER PAINTS THE SUMMER

A smoky rain riddles the ocean plains,
Rings on the beaches' stones, stomps in the swales,
Batters the panes
Of the shore hotel, and the hoped-for summer chills
    and fails.
The summer people sigh,
"Is this July?"

They talk by the lobby fire but no one hears
For the thrum of the rain. In the dim and sounding
    halls,
Din at the ears,
Dark at the eyes well in the head, and the ping-pong
    balls
Scatter their hollow knocks
Like crazy clocks.

But up in his room by artificial light
My father paints the summer, and his brush
Tricks into sight
The prosperous sleep, the girdling stir and clear
    steep hush
Of a summer never seen,
A granted green.

Summer, luxuriant Sahara, the orchard spray
Gales in the Eden trees, the knight again
Can cast away
His burning mail, Rome is at Anzio: but the rain
For the ping-pong's optative bop
Will never stop.

Caught Summer is always an imagined time.
Time gave it, yes, but time out of any mind.
There must be prime
In the heart to beget that season, to reach past rain
    and find
Riding the palest days
Its perfect blaze.

FALLING ASLEEP IN A GARDEN

All day the bees have come to the garden.
They hover, swivel in arcs and, whirling, light
On stamens heavy with pollen, probe and revel
Inside the yellow and red starbursts of dahlias
Or cling to lobelia's blue-white mouths
Or climb the speckled trumpets of foxgloves.

My restless eyes follow their restlessness
As they plunge bodily headfirst into treasure,
Gold-fevered among these horns of plenty.
They circle me, a flowerless patch
With nothing to offer in the way of sweetness
Or light against the first omens of evening.

Some, even now, are dying at the end
Of their few weeks, some being born in the dark,
Some simply waiting for life, but some are dancing
Deep in their hives, telling the hungry
The sun will be that way, the garden this far:
This is the way to the garden. They hum at my ear.

And I wake up, startled, seeing the early
Stars beginning to bud in constellations.
The bees have gathered somewhere like petals closing
For the coming of the cold. The silhouette
Of a sphinx moth swerves to drink at a flowerhead.
The night-blooming moon opens its pale corolla.

DOG-DAYS

A ladder sticking up at the open window,
The top of an old ladder;
And all of Summer is there.

Great waves and tufts of wistaria surge across
    the window,
And a thin, belated blossom
Jerks up and down in the sunlight;
Purple translucence against the blue sky.
"Tie back this branch," I say,
But my hands are sticky with leaves,
And my nostrils widen to the smell of crushed green.
The ladder moves uneasily at the open window,
And I call to the man beneath,
"Tie back that branch."

There is a ladder leaning against the window-sill,
And a mutter of thunder in the air.

AUGUST MOON

Gold like a half-slice of orange
Fished from a stiff Old-Fashioned, the moon
Lolls on the sky that goes deeper blue
By the tick of the watch. Or
Lolls like a real brass button half-buttoned
On the blue flannel sleeve
Of an expensive seagoing blue blazer.

Slowly stars, in a gradual
Eczema of glory, gain definition.

What kind of world is this we walk in?

It makes no sense except
The inner, near-soundless *chug-chug* of the body's
        old business –
Your father's cancer, or
Mother's stroke, or
The cat's fifth pregnancy.

Anyway, while night
Hardens into its infinite being,
We walk down the woods-lane, dreaming
There's an inward means of
Communication with

That world whose darkling susurration
Might – if only we were lucky – be
Deciphered.

Children do not count years
Except at birthday parties.
We count them unexpectedly,
At random, like
A half-wit pulling both triggers
Of a ten-gauge with no target, then
Wondering what made the noise,
Or what hit the shoulder with the flat
Butt of the axe-head.

But this is off the point, which is
The counting of years, and who
Wants to live anyway
Except to be of use to
Somebody loved?

At least, that's what they say.

Do you hear the great owl in distance?

Do you remember a childhood prayer –
A hand on your head?

The moon is lost in tree-darkness.
Stars show now only
In the pale path between treetops.
The track of white gravel leads forward in darkness.

I advise you to hold hands as you walk,
And speak not a word.

BLACKBERRY-PICKING
For Philip Hobsbaum

Late August, given heavy rain and sun
For a full week, the blackberries would ripen.
At first, just one, a glossy purple clot
Among others, red, green, hard as a knot.
You ate that first one and its flesh was sweet
Like thickened wine: summer's blood was in it
Leaving stains upon the tongue and lust for
Picking. Then red ones inked up and that hunger
Sent us out with milk cans, pea tins, jam pots
Where briars scratched and wet grass bleached
        our boots.
Round hayfields, cornfields and potato drills
We trekked and picked until the cans were full,
Until the tinkling bottom had been covered
With green ones, and on top big dark blobs burned
Like a plate of eyes. Our hands were peppered
With thorn pricks, our palms sticky as Bluebeard's.

We hoarded the fresh berries in the byre.
But when the bath was filled we found a fur,
A rat-grey fungus, glutting on our cache.
The juice was stinking too. Once off the bush
The fruit fermented, the sweet flesh would turn sour.
I always felt like crying. It wasn't fair
That all the lovely canfuls smelt of rot.
Each year I hoped they'd keep, knew they would not.

LATE AUGUST ON THE LIDO

To lie on these beaches for another summer
Would not become them at all,
And yet the water and her sands will suffer
When, in the fall,
These golden children will be taken from her.

It is not the gold they bring: enough of that
Has shone in the water for ages
And in the bright theater of Venice at their backs;
But the final stages
Of all those afternoons when they played and sat

And waited for a beckoning wind to blow them
Back over the water again
Are scenes most necessary to this ocean.
What actors then
Will play when these disperse from the sand
    below them?

All this is over until, perhaps, next spring;
This last afternoon must be pleasing.
Europe, Europe is over, but they lie here still,
While the wind, increasing,
Sands teeth, sands eyes, sands taste, sands everything.

HYLA BROOK

By June our brook's run out of song and speed.
Sought for much after that, it will be found
Either to have gone groping underground
(And taken with it all the Hyla breed
That shouted in the mist a month ago,
Like ghost of sleigh-bells in a ghost of snow) –
Or flourished and come up in jewel-weed,
Weak foliage that is blown upon and bent
Even against the way its waters went.
Its bed is left a faded paper sheet
Of dead leaves stuck together by the heat –
A brook to none but who remember long.
This as it will be seen is other far
Than with brooks taken otherwhere in song.
We love the things we love for what they are.

SUMMER IS ENDED

To think that this meaningless thing was ever a rose,
    Scentless, colourless, *this*!
  Will it ever be thus (who knows?)
     Thus with our bliss,
   If we wait till the close?

Tho' we care not to wait for the end, there comes the end
    Sooner, later, at last,
  Which nothing can mar, nothing mend:
     An end locked fast,
   Bent we cannot re-bend.

"AS IMPERCEPTIBLY
AS GRIEF"

As imperceptibly as Grief
The Summer lapsed away –
Too imperceptible at last
To seem like Perfidy.

A Quietness distilled,
As Twilight long begun,
Or Nature, spending with herself
Sequestered Afternoon.

The Dusk drew earlier in –
The Morning foreign shone –
A courteous, yet harrowing Grace,
As Guest who would be gone.

And thus, without a Wing,
Or service of a Keel,
Our Summer made her light escape
Into the Beautiful.

EMILY DICKINSON

"WHEN SUMMER'S END
IS NIGHING"

When summer's end is nighing
    And skies at evening cloud,
I muse on change and fortune
    And all the feats I vowed
    When I was young and proud.

The weathercock at sunset
    Would lose the slanted ray,
And I would climb the beacon
    That looked to Wales away
    And saw the last of day.

From hill and cloud and heaven
    The hues of evening died;
Night welled through lane and hollow
    And hushed the countryside,
    But I had youth and pride.

And I with earth and nightfall
    In converse high would stand,
Late, till the west was ashen
    And darkness hard at hand,
    And the eye lost the land.

The year might age, and cloudy
    The lessening day might close,
But air of other summers
    Breathed from beyond the snows,
    And I had hope of those.

They came and were and are not
    And come no more anew;
And all the years and seasons
    That ever can ensue
    Must now be worse and few.

So here's an end of roaming
    On eves when autumn nighs:
The ear too fondly listens
    For summer's parting sighs,
    And then the heart replies.

AUTUMN

TO AUTUMN

Season of mists and mellow fruitfulness,
    Close bosom-friend of the maturing sun;
Conspiring with him how to load and bless
    With fruit the vines that round the thatch-eaves run;
To bend with apples the mossed cottage-trees,
    And fill all fruit with ripeness to the core;
        To swell the gourd, and plump the hazel shells
    With a sweet kernel; to set budding more,
And still more, later flowers for the bees,
Until they think warm days will never cease,
        For summer has o'er-brimmed their clammy cells.

Who hath not seen thee oft amid thy store?
    Sometimes whoever seeks abroad may find
Thee sitting careless on a granary floor,
    Thy hair soft-lifted by the winnowing wind;
Or on a half-reaped furrow sound asleep,
    Drowsed with the fumes of poppies, while thy hook
        Spares the next swath and all its twinèd flowers:
And sometime like a gleaner thou dost keep
    Steady thy laden head across a brook;
    Or by a cider-press, with patient look,
        Thou watchest the last oozings hours by hours.

123

Where are the songs of spring? Ay, where are they?
   Think not of them, thou hast thy music too, —
While barrèd clouds bloom the soft-dying day,
   And touch the stubble-plains with rosy hue;
Then in a wailful choir the small gnats mourn
   Among the river sallows, borne aloft
      Or sinking as the light wind lives or dies;
And full-grown lambs loud bleat from hilly bourn;
   Hedge-crickets sing; and now with treble soft
   The red-breast whistles from a garden-croft;
      And gathering swallows twitter in the skies.

"SUMMER BEGINS TO HAVE THE LOOK"

Summer begins to have the look
Peruser of enchanting Book
Reluctantly but sure perceives
A gain upon the backward leaves –

Autumn begins to be inferred
By millinery of the cloud
Or deeper color in the shawl
That wraps the everlasting hill.

The eye begins its avarice
A meditation chastens speech
Some Dyer of a distant tree
Resumes his gaudy industry.

Conclusion is the course of All
At *most* to be perennial
And then elude stability
Recalls to immortality.

"FALL, LEAVES, FALL"

Fall, leaves, fall; die, flowers, away;
Lengthen night and shorten day;
Every leaf speaks bliss to me
Fluttering from the autumn tree.
I shall smile when wreaths of snow
Blossom where the rose should grow;
I shall sing when night's decay
Ushers in a drearier day.

UNHARVESTED

A scent of ripeness from over a wall.
And come to leave the routine road
And look for what had made me stall,
There sure enough was an apple tree
That had eased itself of its summer load,
And of all but its trivial foliage free,
Now breathed as light as a lady's fan.
For there there had been an apple fall
As complete as the apple had given man.
The ground was one circle of solid red.

May something go always unharvested!
May much stay out of our stated plan,
Apples or something forgotten and left,
So smelling their sweetness would be no theft.

AUTUMN

There is a wind where the rose was;
Cold rain where sweet grass was;
   And clouds like sheep
   Stream o'er the steep
Grey skies where the lark was.

Nought gold where your hair was;
Nought warm where your hand was;
   But phantom, forlorn,
   Beneath the thorn,
Your ghost where your face was.

Sad winds where your voice was;
Tears, tears where my heart was;
   And ever with me,
   Child, ever with me,
Silence where hope was.

AUTUMN

The thistledown's flying, though the winds are all still,
On the green grass now lying, now mounting the hill,
The spring from the fountain now boils like a pot;
Through stones past the counting it bubbles red-hot.

The ground parched and cracked is like overbaked
    bread,
The greensward all wracked is, bents dried up and dead.
The fallow fields glitter like water indeed,
And gossamers twitter, flung from weed unto weed.

Hill-tops like hot iron glitter bright in the sun,
And the rivers we're eying burn to gold as they run;
Burning hot is the ground, liquid gold is the air;
Whoever looks round sees Eternity there.

JOHN CLARE

AUTUMN

All day I have watched the purple vine leaves
Fall into the water.
And now in the moonlight they still fall,
But each leaf is fringed with silver.

AUTUMN CHANT

Now the autumn shudders
   In the rose's root.
Far and wide the ladders
   Lean among the fruit.

Now the autumn clambers
   Up the trellised frame,
And the rose remembers
   The dust from which it came.

Brighter than the blossom
   On the rose's bough
Sits the wizened, orange,
   Bitter berry now;

Beauty never slumbers;
   All is in her name;
But the rose remembers
   The dust from which it came.

ODE TO THE WEST WIND

I

O wild west wind, thou breath of autumn's being,
Thou from whose unseen presence the leaves dead
Are driven like ghosts from an enchanter fleeing,

Yellow, and black, and pale, and hectic red,
Pestilence-stricken multitudes! O thou
Who chariotest to their dark wintry bed

The wingèd seeds, where they lie cold and low,
Each like a corpse within its grave, until
Thine azure sister of the spring shall blow

Her clarion o'er the dreaming earth, and fill
(Driving sweet buds like flocks to feed in air)
With living hues and odours plain and hill:

Wild spirit, which art moving everywhere;
Destroyer and preserver; hear, O hear!

II

Thou on whose stream, 'mid the steep sky's commotion,
Loose clouds like earth's decaying leaves are shed,
Shook from the tangled boughs of heaven and ocean,

Angels of rain and lightning: there are spread
On the blue surface of thine airy surge,
Like the bright hair uplifted from the head

Of some fierce Maenad, even from the dim verge
Of the horizon to the zenith's height,
The locks of the approaching storm. Thou dirge

Of the dying year, to which this closing night
Will be the dome of a vast sepulchre,
Vaulted with all thy congregated might

Of vapours, from whose solid atmosphere
Black rain, and fire, and hail will burst: O hear!

III

Thou who didst waken from his summer dreams
The blue Mediterranean, where he lay,
Lulled by the coil of his crystalline streams,

Beside a pumice isle in Baiae's bay,
And saw in sleep old palaces and towers
Quivering within the wave's intenser day,

All overgrown with azure moss and flowers
So sweet, the sense faints picturing them! Thou
For whose path the Atlantic's level powers

Cleave themselves into chasms, while far below
The sea-blooms and the oozy woods which wear
The sapless foliage of the ocean, know

Thy voice, and suddenly grow gray with fear,
And tremble and despoil themselves: O hear!

IV

If I were a dead leaf thou mightest bear;
If I were a swift cloud to fly with thee;
A wave to pant beneath thy power, and share

The impulse of thy strength, only less free
Than thou, O uncontrollable! if even
I were as in my boyhood, and could be

The comrade of thy wanderings over heaven,
As then, when to outstrip thy skiey speed
Scarce seemed a vision; I would ne'er have striven

As thus with thee in prayer in my sore need.
O! lift me as a wave, a leaf, a cloud!
I fall upon the thorns of life! I bleed!

A heavy weight of hours has chained and bowed
One too like thee: tameless, and swift, and proud.

V

Make me thy lyre, even as the forest is:
What if my leaves are falling like its own?
The tumult of thy mighty harmonies

Will take from both a deep autumnal tone,
Sweet though in sadness. Be thou, spirit fierce,
My spirit! Be thou me, impetuous one!

Drive my dead thoughts over the universe,
Like withered leaves, to quicken a new birth;
And, by the incantation of this verse,

Scatter, as from an unextinguished hearth
Ashes and sparks, my words among mankind!
Be through my lips to unawakened earth

The trumpet of a prophecy! O wind,
If winter comes, can spring be far behind?

THE SEVEN SORROWS

The first sorrow of autumn
Is the slow goodbye
Of the garden who stands so long in the evening –
A brown poppy head,
The stalk of a lily,
And still cannot go.

The second sorrow
Is the empty feet
Of the pheasant who hangs from a hook with his
        brothers.
The woodland of gold
Is folded in feathers
With its head in a bag.

And the third sorrow
Is the slow goodbye
Of the sun who has gathered the birds and who
        gathers
The minutes of evening,
The golden and holy
Ground of the picture.

The fourth sorrow
Is the pond gone black
Ruined and sunken the city of water –

The beetle's palace,
The catacombs
Of the dragonfly.

And the fifth sorrow
Is the slow goodbye
Of the woodland that quietly breaks up its camp.
One day it's gone.
It has left only litter –
Firewood, tentpoles.

And the sixth sorrow
Is the fox's sorrow
The joy of the huntsman, the joy of the hounds,
The hooves that pound
Till earth closes her ear
To the fox's prayer.

And the seventh sorrow
Is the slow goodbye
Of the face with its wrinkles that looks through the
    window
As the year packs up
Like a tatty fairground
That came for the children.

TED HUGHES

AN AUTUMN SUNSET

I

Leaguered in fire
The wild black promontories of the coast extend
Their savage silhouettes;
The sun in universal carnage sets,
And, halting higher,
The motionless storm-clouds mass their sullen
     threats,
Like an advancing mob in sword-points penned,
That, balked, yet stands at bay.
Mid-zenith hangs the fascinated day
In wind-lustrated hollows crystalline,
A wan Valkyrie whose wide pinions shine
Across the ensanguined ruins of the fray,
And in her hand swings high o'erhead,
Above the waste of war,
The silver torch-light of the evening star
Wherewith to search the faces of the dead.

II

Lagooned in gold,
Seem not those jetty promontories rather
The outposts of some ancient land forlorn,
Uncomforted of morn,
Where old oblivions gather,

The melancholy unconsoling fold
Of all things that go utterly to death
And mix no more, no more
With life's perpetually awakening breath?
Shall Time not ferry me to such a shore,
Over such sailless seas,
To walk with hope's slain importunities
In miserable marriage? Nay, shall not
All things be there forgot,
Save the sea's golden barrier and the black
Close-crouching promontories?
Dead to all shames, forgotten of all glories,
Shall I not wander there, a shadow's shade,
A spectre self-destroyed,
So purged of all remembrance and sucked back
Into the primal void,
That should we on that shore phantasmal meet
I should not know the coming of your feet?

EDITH WHARTON

AUTUMN
(A Fragment)

What doth the drowsing mind not then conceive?

— DERZHAVIN

I

It is October, and the lingering leaves
Are disappearing from the naked branches;
The road is glazed, the cold of autumn breathes;
The millstream still sounds loudly as it passes,
But now the pond is hard; out to the fields
My neighbour promptly leads his canine forces;
The frenzied sport lays waste the winter crops,
The sleeping groves are roused by baying dogs.

II

This is my season: Spring is quite the worst,
I hate the thaw, it makes me ill – stench, mire,
The blood is in a ferment, I am depressed.
The sternness of Midwinter I prefer;
How I love its snows, when free and fast
The sled speeds on beneath the evening star,
When she beside you gives your hand a squeeze,
Warm beneath fur, fresh, trembling and ablaze!

140

III

What a delight, to glide on fine sharp steel
Over the crystal river, far from shore!
The sparkle of a Winter festival! . . .
But snow, when it has fallen half the year,
Inevitably loses its appeal,
Even for that deep burrower, the bear.
One can't forever ride with young Armidas
Or mope by stoves in front of double windows.

IV

Glorious Summer! You I should love best
But for your dust and flies and scorching heat.
You torture us, destroy our faculties;
Like earth, we suffer drought, our only thought –
How we can satisfy our raging thirst.
The passing of Dame Winter we regret;
We saw her off with fruit liqueur and blinis,
And now we fête her with ice-cream and ice.

V

Autumn, I know, is commonly berated:
That sentiment, dear reader, isn't mine;
I love it for its quietly glowing beauty.

As to a child unloved by its own kin,
I am distinctly drawn to it – yes, Autumn,
Of all the seasons, is my favourite one.
I am no vainglorious lover: truth to tell,
My love of it has something whimsical.

VI

How can I explain? It has for me
Something of the quality you'll find
In a consumptive girl; condemned to die,
The poor thing wanes, meekly, without complaint.
On her thin lips a smile is visible;
She is unconscious of the yawning ground;
Her wasted face is shot with hectic tone.
Alive today, tomorrow she is gone.

VII

Season of melancholy! Eye's enchanter!
How pleasing to me are your farewell hues –
How I love the pomp of fading Nature,
The trees arrayed in gold-vermilion dress,
The fresh wind blowing through their tops and
        chanting,
The dense and darkly undulating skies,
The sun's infrequent ray, the early frost,
And grizzled Winter's lightly murmured threats.

VIII

Every year, when Autumn comes, I flourish;
The Russian cold is good for my well-being;
In forms of daily life I take new relish,
So that sleep duly comes, and duly hunger;
The blood runs through my heart in pleasant rush,
Desires seethe – I am happy again, and young
And full of life – such is my organism
(If you'll forgive a vulgar prosaism).

IX

My mount is brought; over the open heath
It bears its rider on with flying mane;
Resoundingly beneath each flashing hoof
The cracking ice rings out from solid ground.
The brief day fades, in the forgotten hearth
A fire is burning once again – in turn
It leaps, dies down; in front of it I read
Or lose myself to lengthy spells of thought.

X

And I forget the world, and in sweet peace
I am sweetly lulled by imagination;
And now the muse of poetry appears:
My soul is caught in lyrical confusion,
It trembles, sounds, and seeks, as if in dream,
And overflows in unrestrained expression –

And I am visited by unseen guests,
Acquaintance from oblivion, fancy's fruits.

XI

Into my mind ambitious thoughts come swarming,
And rhymes race out to meet them on the way,
My fingers reach for a pen, the pen for paper,
And in a moment, verses freely flow.
So a ship sleeps, immobile in the water,
Till suddenly, forward run the sailors – high
And low they clamber – wind fills out the sails;
The giant moves, and soon she cleaves the waves.

XII

She sails. But where are *we* to sail? . . .

SIMPLE AUTUMNAL

The measured blood beats out the year's delay.
The tearless eyes and heart, forbidden grief,
Watch the burned, restless, but abiding leaf,
The brighter branches arming the bright day.

The cone, the curving fruit should fall away,
The vine stem crumble, ripe grain know its sheaf.
Bonded to time, fires should have done, be brief,
But, serfs to sleep, they glitter and they stay.

Because not last nor first, grief in its prime
Wakes in the day, and hears of life's intent.
Sorrow would break the seal stamped over time
And set the baskets where the bough is bent.

Full season's come, yet filled trees keep the sky
And never scent the ground where they must lie.

THE FLUX OF AUTUMN

All is a golden burst, the wind burning
The golden trees that plunge
Headmost into the burning light and make
A sound as fierce as waterfalls –
Excitable air of dying changes,
Autumn of the year and of the height!

So I by shady walking saw old leaves
Whirled in hardy rings and circles plunged,
Gyration of the fire-plagued spirits crying!
And saw it was a fight to the death this year,
The fortress mountains thinning their own shapes,
Advancing now from thickets of the sense,
From wayward, tall, exultant, sap-choked green,
A hardy brambled green that founders us,
Into this umber, somber, earth-dark thing
That then at twilight imitates a blue
And in a link, a series, and a bare earth-warded
Chain sets up the gaunter distances
Between their star-reefed differences and us.

What is this dream we make with leaf-rained earth
Or do we live upon a fire not ours
Like absentees of will, Undines of fantasies
Waiting and listening in a rich suspense

Expecting half our dreams to be its selves
And all of what we love our own?
So then the reddening apple is as much germane
And those tuft-headed grasses of the field
Rising above their lower-lying kin
And how they are is how they stand
Leaning upon the wind that moves the mind
To lean upon the same all-mothering stuff
And draw the intricate world more close

Until we'd think the rudest empire of tough chaff
       and rock
The very form of our subjective wish
Reshaped again within the restless eye
That takes its bearings from the true itself
To enter then on changes of its being,
A changeless changing, transformings into
An ethereal storming, freshening, continuous,

For I have heard those voices rough
As shaggy earth and humming with the earth's
       own tilth
Or mad as water hurled against a stone
So now you remnant butterfly whose motion makes
A silent music, repeat, repeat,

147

And you thin clouds who deepen in the skies
Your soundlessness against the surged uproar
Until the four winds seem to swell one tone
From out the banter between field and wood
To let us think all things are full of gods.

As shadow falls upon a rock.
The shadow of a bird has crossed my heart
That we are these, these living things, enough!
By them we make a burning territory
Wherein there walk those influences of sky
At that long moment of the eye
When all leaps upward at some ancient wind
Blown from the corners of some leaf-blocked road
We walk upon in sober truth. To be so caught
By all this phantomed streaming forth
It seems a greater phantom is at work.

Quick-shading now, the battle of leaves,
The airy-quick, a gusty lunging, throbbing,
Metallic clangor, pipes, the errant horn.
Misled by fevers then, by ditches lost,
By fireweed and the hawks that plunge,
This that I'm in's become a changeling cloud.
The clarity of mountains is obscured
By what we'd fortify that must be dreamed.
Old territory mapped and walked

Nightly, daily, in the impetuous eye
Of thought.
                    Until the dream's walked out.

"TURN ME TO MY YELLOW LEAVES"

Turn me to my yellow leaves,
I am better satisfied;
There is nothing in me grieves –
That was never born – and died.
Let me be a scarlet flame
On a windy autumn morn,
I, who never had a name,
Nor from a breathing image born.
From the margin let me fall
Where the farthest stars sink down.
And the void consume me, – all
Into nothingness to drown.
Let me dream my dream entire,
Withered as an autumn leaf –
Let me have my vain desire,
Vain – as it is brief!

THE LATTER RAIN

The latter rain, it falls in anxious haste
Upon the sun-dried fields and branches bare,
Loosening with searching drops the rigid waste
As if it would each root's lost strength repair;
But not a blade grows green as in the spring,
No swelling twig puts forth its thickening leaves;
The robins only mid the harvests sing
Pecking the grain that scatters from the sheaves;
The rain falls still – the fruit all ripened drops,
It pierces chestnut burr and walnut shell,
The furrowed fields disclose the yellow crops,
Each bursting pod of talents used can tell,
And all that once received the early rain
Declare to man it was not sent in vain.

JONES VERY

TO AUTUMN

O Autumn, laden with fruit, and stained
With the blood of the grape, pass not, but sit
Beneath my shady roof; there thou mayest rest,
And tune thy jolly voice to my fresh pipe;
And all the daughters of the year shall dance!
Sing now the lusty song of fruits and flowers.

"The narrow bud opens her beauties to
The sun, and love runs in her thrilling veins;
Blossoms hang round the brows of morning, and
Flourish down the bright cheek of modest eve,
Till clust'ring Summer breaks forth into singing,
And feather'd clouds strew flowers round her head.

"The spirits of the air live on the smells
Of fruit; and joy, with pinions light, roves round
The gardens, or sits singing in the trees."
Thus sang the jolly Autumn as he sat;
Then rose, girded himself, and o'er the bleak
Hills fled from our sight; but left his golden load.

HOAR-FROST

In the cloud-gray mornings
I heard the herons flying;
And when I came into my garden,
My silken outer-garment
Trailed over withered leaves.
A dried leaf crumbles at a touch,
But I have seen many Autumns
With herons blowing like smoke
Across the sky.

AMY LOWELL

153

WRITTEN IN AUTUMN

O Autumn! how I love thy pensive air,
   Thy yellow garb, thy visage sad and dun!
   When from the misty east the labouring sun
Bursts through thy fogs, that gathering round
     him, dare
Obscure his beams, which, though enfeebled, dart
   On the cold, dewy plains a lustre bright:
   But chief, the sounds of thy reft woods delight;
Their deep, low murmurs to my soul impart
A solemn stillness, while they seem to speak
   Of Spring, of Summer now for ever past,
   Of drear, approaching Winter, and the blast
Which shall ere long their soothing quiet break:
   Here, when for faded joys my heaving breast
   Throbs with vain pangs, here will I love to rest.

THE FALL OF THE LEAF

Grown tired of this rank summer's wealth,
    Its raw and superficial show,
I fain would hie away by stealth
    Where no roads meet, but still 't doth trivial grow.

A sober mind will walk alone,
    Apart from nature if need be,
And only its own seasons own,
    For nature having its humanity.

Sometimes a late autumnal thought
    Has crossed my mind in green July,
And to its early freshness brought
    Late ripen'd fruits and an autumnal sky.

A dry but golden thought which gleamed
    Athwart the greenness of my mind,
And prematurely wise it seemed,
    Too ripe 'mid summer's youthful bowers to find.

So have I seen one yellow leaf
    Amid the glossy leaves of June,
Which pensive hung, though not with grief,
    Like some fair flower, it had changed so soon.

I scent my med'cine from afar,
    Where the rude simpler of the year
October leads the rustling war,
    And strews his honors on the summer's bier.

The evening of the year draws on,
    The fields a later aspect wear,
Since summer's garishness is gone,
    Some grains of night tincture the noontide air.

Behold the shadows of the trees
    Now circle wider 'bout their stem,
Like sentries which by slow degrees
    Perform their rounds, gently protecting them.

And as the season doth decline
    The sun affords a scantier light,
Behind each needle of the pine
    There lurks a small auxiliar of the night.

After each shrub and straggling fence
    That marks the meadow's pensive green,
And shows the meadow's opulence,
    Evening's insidious foot at noon is seen.

Wave upon wave a mellower air
    Flows over all the region,

As if there were some tincture there
    Of ripeness caught from the long summer's sun.

I hear the cricket's slumbrous lay
    Around, beneath me, and on high,
It rocks the night, it lulls the day,
    And everywhere 'tis nature's lullaby.

But most he chirps beneath the sod,
    Where he hath made his winter's bed,
His creak grown fainter, but more broad,
    A film of autumn o'er the summer spread.

Upon my bed at early dawn
    I hear the cocks proclaim the day,
Though the moon shines serenely on
    As if her queenly course they could not stay;

Nor pull her down with their faint din
    From riding at that lofty height,
Who in her shining knows no sin,
    But is unconscious of a nobler light.

The stars withhold their shining not
    Or singly or in scattered crowds,
But seem like Parthian arrows shot
    By yielding night 'mid the advancing clouds.

And has time got so forward then?
From what perennial fount of joy
Do ye inspire the hearts of men,
And teach them how the daylight to employ?

From your abundance pray impart,
Who dost so freely spill,
Some bravery unto my heart,
Or let me taste of thy perennial rill.

Small birds in fleets migrating by
Now beat across some meadow's bay,
And as they tack and veer on high,
With faint and hurried click beguile the way.

The moon is ripe fruit in the sky
Which overhangs her harvest now,
The sun doth break his stem well nigh
From summer's height he has declined so low.

The greedy earth doth pluck his fruit,
And cast it in night's lap,
The stars more brightly glisten, mute
Though their tears be, to see their lord's mishap.

The harvest rattles in the wind,
Ripe apples overhang the hay,

The cereal flavor of my mind
  Natheless, tells me I am as ripe as they.

I hearing get who had but ears,
  And sight who had but eyes before,
I moments live who lived but years,
  And truth discern who knew but learning's lore.

Far in the woods these golden days
  Some leaf obeys its maker's call,
And through their hollow aisles it plays
  With delicate touch the prelude of the fall.

Gently withdrawing from its stem
  It lightly lays itself along,
Where the same hand hath pillowed them
  Resigned to sleep upon the old year's throng.

The loneliest birch is brown and sere,
  The farthest pool is strewn with leaves,
Which float upon their watery bier,
  Where is no eye that sees, no heart that grieves.

I marked when first the wind grew rude
  Each leaf curled like a living thing,
As if with the ripe air it would
  Secure some faint memorial of the spring.

Then for its sake it turned a boat
   And dared new elements to brave,
A painted palace which did float
   A summer's hoarded wealth to save.

Oh could I catch these sounds remote,
   Could I preserve to human ear,
The strains which on the breezes float,
   And sing the requiem of the dying year.

I stood beside an oaken copse
   When the first gale of autumn sighed,
It gently waved the birch tree tops
   Then rustled the oak leaves and died.

But not the strains which it awoke,
   For in my inmost sense I hear
The melody of which it spoke
   Still faintly rising on my inward ear.

A ripple on the river fell,
   A shadow o'er the landscape passed,
And still the whispering ferns could tell
   Whither the stranger travelled so fast.

How stand the cottages of men
   In these so fair October days,

Along the wood along the fen
   I see them looming through the mellow haze.

Immersed in Nature there they lie
   Against some cliff or chestnut's shade
Scarce obvious to the traveller's eye
   Who thoughtful traverses the forest glade.

The harvest lies about the door
   The chestnut drops its burs around
As if they were the stock that bore
   The yellow crops that strew the ground.

The lily loves the river's tide
   The meadows are the daisy's haunt
The aspens on the mountain side
   Here child of nature grows the human plant.

The jay screams through the chestnut wood
   The crisped and yellow leaves around
Are hue and texture of my mood,
   And these rough burs my heirlooms on the ground.

The threadbare trees so poor and thin
   They are no wealthier than I,
But with as brave a core within
   They rear their boughs to the October sky.

Poor knights they are which bravely wait
   The charge of winter's cavalry,
Keeping a simple Roman state
   Discumbered of their Persian luxury.

Thank God who seasons thus the year
   And sometimes kindly slants his rays,
For in his winter he's most near
   And plainest seen upon the shortest days.

Who gently tempers now his heats
   And then his harsher cold, lest we
Should surfeit on the summer's sweets,
   Or pine upon the winter's crudity.

AUTUMN REFRAIN

The skreak and skritter of evening gone
And grackles gone and sorrows of the sun,
The sorrows of sun, too, gone ... the moon and moon,
The yellow moon of words about the nightingale
In measureless measures, not a bird for me
But the name of a bird and the name of a nameless air
I have never – shall never hear. And yet beneath
The stillness of everything gone, and being still,
Being and sitting still, something resides,
Some skreaking and skrittering residuum,
And grates these evasions of the nightingale
Though I have never – shall never hear that bird.
And the stillness is in the key, all of it is,
The stillness is all in the key of that desolate sound.

THE DYING GARDEN

The flowers get a darkening brilliance now;
And in the still sun-heated air stand out
As stars and soloists where they had been before
Choruses and choirs; at the equinox,
I mean, when the great gyroscope begins
To spin the sun under the line and do
Harvest together with fall: the time that trees
Crimp in their steepled shapes, the hand of leaf
Become a claw; when wealth and death are one,
When moth and wasp and mouse come in the house
For comfort if they can; the deepening time
When sketchy Orion begins his slow cartwheel
About the southern sky, the time of turn
When moth and wasp and mouse come in the house
To die there as they may; and there will be,
You know, All Saints, All Souls, and Halloween,
The killing frost, the end of Daylight Time,
Sudden the nightfall on the afternoon
And on children scuffling home through drifts of leaf;
Till you drop the pumpkins on the compost heap,
The blackened jack o'lanterns with their candled eyes,
And in the darkening garden turn for home
Through summer's flowers now all gone, withdrawn,
The four o'clocks, the phlox, the hollyhocks,
Somber November in amber and umber embering out.

AN AUTUMNAL

The lichens, like a gorgeous, soft disease
        In rust and gold rosette
Emboss the bouldered wall, and creepers seize
        In their cup-footed fret,

Ravelled and bare, such purchase as affords.
        The sap-tide slides to ebb,
And leafstems, like the drumsticks of small birds,
        Lie snagged in a spiderweb.

Down at the stonework base, among the stump-
        Fungus and feather moss,
Dead leaves are sunken in a shallow sump
        Of energy and loss,

Enriched now with the colors of old coins
        And brilliance of wet leather.
An earthen tea distills at the roots-groins
        Into the smoky weather

A deep, familiar essence of the year:
        A sweet fetor, a ghost
Of foison, gently welcoming us near
        To humus, mulch, compost.

The last mosquitoes lazily hum and play
     Above the yeasting earth
A feeble *Gloria* to this cool decay
     Or casual dirge of birth.

AFTERMATH

When the summer fields are mown,
When the birds are fledged and flown,
   And the dry leaves strew the path;
With the falling of the snow,
With the cawing of the crow,
Once again the fields we mow
   And gather in the aftermath.

Not the sweet, new grass with flowers
Is this harvesting of ours;
   Not the upland clover bloom;
But the rowen mixed with weeds,
Tangled tufts from marsh and meads,
Where the poppy drops its seeds
   In the silence and the gloom.

THE LOVE FOR OCTOBER

A child looking at ruins grows younger
but cold
and wants to wake to a new name
I have been younger in October
than in all the months of spring
walnut and may leaves the color
of shoulders at the end of summer
a month that has been to the mountain
and become light there
the long grass lies pointing uphill
even in death for a reason
that none of us knows
and the wren laughs in the early shade now
come again shining glance in your good time
naked air late morning
my love is for lightness
of touch foot feather
the day is yet one more yellow leaf
and without turning I kiss the light
by an old well on the last of the month
gathering wild rose hips
in the sun

OCTOBER DAWN

October is marigold, and yet
A glass half full of wine left out

To the dark heaven all night, by dawn
Has dreamed a premonition

Of ice across its eye as if
The ice-age had begun its heave.

The lawn overtrodden and strewn
From the night before, and the whistling green

Shrubbery are doomed. Ice
Has got its spearhead into place.

First a skin, delicately here
Restraining a ripple from the air;

Soon plate and rivet on pond and brook;
Then tons of chain and massive lock

To hold rivers. Then, sound by sight
Will Mammoth and Sabre-tooth celebrate

Reunion while a fist of cold
Squeezes the fire at the core of the world,

Squeezes the fire at the core of the heart,
And now it is about to start.

OCTOBER

Bending above the spicy woods which blaze,
Arch skies so blue they flash, and hold the sun
Immeasurably far; the waters run
Too slow, so freighted are the river-ways
With gold of elms and birches from the maze
Of forests. Chestnuts, clicking one by one,
Escape from satin burs; her fringes done,
The gentian spreads them out in sunny days,
And, like late revelers at dawn, the chance
Of one sweet, mad, last hour, all things assail,
And conquering, flush and spin; while, to enhance
The spell, by sunset door, wrapped in a veil
Of red and purple mists, the summer, pale,
Steals back alone for one more song and dance.

HELEN HUNT JACKSON

LAST WEEK IN OCTOBER

The trees are undressing, and fling in many places –
On the gray road, the roof, the window-sill –
Their radiant robes and ribbons and yellow laces;
A leaf each second so is flung at will,
Here, there, another and another, still and still.

A spider's web has caught one while downcoming,
That stays there dangling when the rest pass on;
Like a suspended criminal hangs he, mumming
In golden garb, while one yet green, high yon,
Trembles, as fearing such a fate for himself anon.

END OF OCTOBER

Leaves wait as the reversal of wind
comes to a stop. The stopped woods
are seized of quiet; waiting for rain
bird & bug conversations stutter to
a stop.
Between the road
and the car in the road and me in the car,
and the woods
and the forms standing tall and the broken
forms and the small forms that crawl there,
the rain begins to fall. Rain-strands,
thin slips of vertical rivers, roll
the shredded waters out of the cloud
and dump them puddling to the ground.
Like sticks half-drowned the trees
lean so my eyes snap some into
lightning shapes, bent & bent.
I leave the car to see where, lower,
the leaves of the shrubs beaten goldleaf
huddle together. In some spaces
nothing but rain appears.

Whatever crosses over
through the wall of rain
changes; old leaves are

now gold. The wall is
continuous, doorless. True,
to get past this wall
there's no need for a door
since it closes around me
as I go through.

HEART OF AUTUMN

Wind finds the northwest gap, fall comes.
Today, under gray cloud-scud and over gray
Wind-flicker of forest, in perfect formation, wild geese
Head for a land of warm water, the *boom*, the lead pellet.

Some crumple in air, fall. Some stagger, recover
    control,
Then take the last glide for a far glint of water. None
Knows what has happened. Now, today, watching
How tirelessly *V* upon *V* arrows the season's logic,

Do I know my own story? At least, they know
When the hour comes for the great wing-beat.
    Sky-strider,
Star-strider — they rise, and the imperial utterance,
Which cries out for distance, quivers in the
    wheeling sky.

That much they know, and in their nature know
The path of pathlessness, with all the joy
Of destiny fulfilling its own name.
I have known time and distance, but not why I am here.

Path of logic, path of folly, all
The same — and I stand, my face lifted now skyward,

Hearing the high beat, my arms outstretched in
     the tingling
Process of transformation, and soon tough legs,

With folded feet, trail in the sounding vacuum
     of passage,
And my heart is impacted with a fierce impulse
To unwordable utterance –
Toward sunset, at a great height.

NO!

No sun – no moon!
No morn – no noon –
No dawn – no dusk – no proper time of day –
No sky – no earthly view –
No distance looking blue –
No road – no street – no "t'other side the way" –
No end to any Row –
No indications where the Crescents go –
No top to any steeple –
No recognitions of familiar people –
No courtesies for showing 'em –
No knowing 'em –
No travelling at all – no locomotion,
No inkling of the way – no notion –
"No go" – by land or ocean –
No mail – no post –
No news from any foreign coast –
No Park – no Ring – no afternoon gentility –
No company – no nobility –
No warmth, no cheerfulness, no healthful ease,
No comfortable feel in any member –
No shade, no shine, no butterflies, no bees,
No fruits, no flowers, no leaves, no birds, –
November!

THOMAS HOOD

NOVEMBER
Impression

A weft of leafless spray
Woven fine against the gray
Of the autumnal day,
And blurred along those ghostly garden tops
Clusters of berries crimson as the drops
That my heart bleeds when I remember
How often, in how many a far November,
Of childhood and my children's childhood I was glad,
With the wild rapture of the Fall,
Of all the beauty, and of all
The ruin, now so intolerably sad.

NOVEMBER

Away with vanity of Man.
   Now comes to visit here
The Maiden Aunt, the Puritan,
   The Spinster of the year.

She likes a world that's furnished plain,
   A sky that's clean and bare,
And garments eminently sane
   For her consistent wear.

Let others deck them as they please
   In frill and furbelow.
She scorns alike the fripperies
   Of flowers and of snow.

Her very speech is shrewd and slight,
   With innuendoes done;
And all of her is hard, thin light
   Or shadow sharp as sun.

Indifferent to the drifting leaf,
   And innocent of guile,
She scarcely knows there dwells a brief
   Enchantment in her smile.

So love her with a sparing love.
    That is her private fashion,
Who fears the August ardor of
    A demonstrated passion.

Yet love her somewhat. It is meet,
    And for our own defense,
After October to find sweet
    Her chilly common sense.

NOVEMBER NIGHT

Listen.
With faint dry sound,
Like steps of passing ghosts,
The leaves, frost-crisp'd, break from the trees
And fall.

LATE NOVEMBER

The white sun
like a moth
on a string
circles the southpole.

DURING WIND AND RAIN

They sing their dearest songs –
He, she, all of them – yea,
Treble and tenor and bass,
    And one to play;
With the candles mooning each face....
    Ah, no; the years O!
How the sick leaves reel down in throngs!

They clear the creeping moss –
Elders and juniors – aye,
Making the pathway neat
    And the garden gay;
And they build a shady seat....
    Ah, no; the years, the years;
See, the white storm-birds wing across!

They are blithely breakfasting all –
Men and maidens – yea,
Under the summer tree,
    With a glimpse of the bay,
While pet fowl come to the knee....
    Ah, no; the years O!
And the rotten rose is ript from the wall.

They change to a high new house,
He, she, all of them – aye,
Clocks and carpets, and chairs
    On the lawn all day,
And brightest things that are theirs....
    Ah, no; the years, the years;
Down their carved names the rain-drop ploughs.

CROW'S NESTS

That lofty stand of trees beyond the field,
Which in the storms of summer stood revealed

As a great fleet of galleons bound our way
Across a moiled expanse of tossing hay,

Full-rigged and swift, and to the topmost sail
Taking their fill and pleasure of the gale,

Now, in this leafless time, are ships no more,
Though it would not be hard to take them for

A roadstead full of naked mast and spar
In which we see now where the crow's nests are.

SPRING AND FALL
To a Young Child

Márgarét, áre you gríeving
Over Goldengrove unleaving?
Leáves, líke the things of man, you
With your fresh thoughts care for, can you?
Áh! ás the heart grows older
It will come to such sights colder
By and by, nor spare a sigh
Though worlds of wanwood leafmeal lie;
And yet you *will* weep and know why.
Now no matter, child, the name:
Sórrow's spríngs áre the same.
Nor mouth had, no nor mind, expressed
What heart heard of, ghost guessed:
It ís the blight man was born for,
It is Margaret you mourn for.

AN OLD-FASHIONED SONG
(Nous n'irons plus au bois)

No more walks in the wood:
The trees have all been cut
Down, and where once they stood
Not even a wagon rut
Appears along the path
Low brush is taking over.

No more walks in the wood;
This is the aftermath
Of afternoons in the clover
Fields where we once made love
Then wandered home together
Where the trees arched above,
Where we made our own weather
When branches were the sky.
Now they are gone for good,
And you, for ill, and I
Am only a passer-by.

We and the trees and the way
Back from the fields of play
Lasted as long as we could.
No more walks in the wood.

JOHN HOLLANDER

"THAT TIME OF YEAR THOU MAYST IN ME BEHOLD"

That time of year thou mayst in me behold
When yellow leaves, or none, or few, do hang
Upon those boughs which shake against the cold,
Bare ruined choirs where late the sweet birds sang.
In me thou seest the twilight of such day
As after sunset fadeth in the west,
Which by and by black night doth take away,
Death's second self, that seals up all in rest.
In me thou seest the glowing of such fire
That on the ashes of his youth doth lie,
As the deathbed whereon it must expire,
Consumed with that which it was nourished by.
   This thou perceivest, which makes thy love
      more strong,
    To love that well which thou must leave ere long.

⌐l(a⌐

l(a

le
af
fa

ll

s)
one
l

iness

WINTER

WINTER

When icicles hang by the wall,
    And Dick the shepherd blows his nail,
And Tom bears logs into the hall,
    And milk comes frozen home in pail,
When blood is nipped, and ways be foul,
Then nightly sings the staring owl,
      Tu-whit, tu-who! A merry note,
      While greasy Joan doth keel the pot.

When all around the wind doth blow,
    And coughing drowns the parson's saw,
And birds sit brooding in the snow,
    And Marian's nose looks red and raw,
When roasted crabs hiss in the bowl,
Then nightly sings the staring owl,
      Tu-whit, tu-who! A merry note,
      While greasy Joan doth keel the pot.

WILLIAM SHAKESPEARE

WINTER

The wrathful winter, 'proaching on apace,
  With blust'ring blasts had all ybared the treen:
And old Saturnus, with his frosty face,
  With chilling cold had pierced the tender green,
  The mantles rent, wherein enwrappèd been
    The gladsome groves that now lay overthrown,
    The tapets torn, and every bloom down blown.

The soil, that erst so seemly was to seen,
  Was all despoilèd of her beauty's hue;
And soot fresh flowers, wherewith the summer's queen
  Had clad the earth, now Boreas' blasts down blew:
  And small fowls flocking, in their song did rue
    The winter's wrath, wherewith each thing defaced
    In woeful wise bewailed the summer past.

Hawthorn had lost his motley livery,
  The naked twigs were shivering all for cold,
And dropping down the tears abundantly.
  Each thing, methought, with weeping eye me told
  The cruel season, bidding me withhold
    Myself within; for I was gotten out
    Into the fields, whereas I walked about. . . .

And sorrowing I, to see the summer flowers,
   The lively green, the lusty leas, forlorn;
The sturdy trees so shattered with the showers,
   The fields so fade, that flourished so beforne:
   It taught me well, all earthly things be born
      To die the death; for nought long time may last:
      The summer's beauty yields to winter's blast.

"IT SIFTS FROM
LEADEN SIEVES"

It sifts from Leaden Sieves –
It powders all the Wood –
It fills with alabaster Wool
The Wrinkles of the Road.

It makes an Even Face
Of Mountain and of Plain –
Unbroken Forehead from the East
Unto the East again.

It reaches to the Fence –
It wraps it, rail by rail,
Till it is lost in Fleeces –
It flings a Crystal Veil

On Stump and Stack and Stem –
The Summer's empty Room,
Acres of Seams where Harvests were,
Recordless, but for them.

It ruffles Wrists of Posts,
As Ankles of a queen –
Then stills its Artisans like Ghosts,
Denying they have been.

"PRAY TO WHAT EARTH DOES THIS SWEET COLD BELONG"

    Pray to what earth does this sweet cold belong,
Which asks no duties and no conscience?
The moon goes up by leaps her cheerful path
In some far summer stratum of the sky,
While stars with their cold shine bedot her way.
The fields gleam mildly back upon the sky,
And far and near upon the leafless shrubs
The snow dust still emits a silvery light.
Under the hedge, where drift banks are their screen,
The titmice now pursue their downy dreams,
As often in the sweltering summer nights
The bee doth drop asleep in the flower cup,
When evening overtakes him with his load.
By the brooksides, in the still genial night,
The more adventurous wanderer may hear
The crystals shoot and form, and winter slow
Increase his rule by gentlest summer means.

WINTER

Cold, moist, young phlegmy Winter now doth lie
In swaddling clouts, like newborn infancy,
Bound up with frosts, and furred with hail and snows,
And like an infant, still it taller grows;
December is my first, and now the sun
To th' Southward tropic, his swift race doth run:
This month he's housed in horned Capricorn,
From thence he 'gins to length the shortned morn,
Through Christendom with great festivity,
Now's held (but guest), for blest Nativity.
Cold frozen January next comes in,
Chilling the blood and shrinking up the skin;
In Aquarius now keeps the long wisht sun,
And Northward his unwearied course doth run:
The day much longer then it was before,
The cold not lessened, but augmented more.
Now toes and ears, and fingers often freeze,
And travelers their noses sometimes leese.
Moist snowy February is my last,
I care not how the winter time doth haste.
In Pisces now the golden sun doth shine,
And Northward still approaches to the line,
The rivers 'gin to ope, the snows to melt,
And some warm glances from his face are felt;
Which is increased by the lengthened day,

Until by's heat, he drive all cold away,
And thus the year in circle runneth round:
Where first it did begin, in th' end it's found.

"THE NIGHT IS FREEZING FAST"

The night is freezing fast,
   To-morrow comes December;
     And winterfalls of old
Are with me from the past;
   And chiefly I remember
     How Dick would hate the cold.

Fall, winter, fall; for he,
   Prompt hand and headpiece clever,
     Has woven a winter robe,
And made of earth and sea
   His overcoat for ever,
     And wears the turning globe.

WINTER WALK

The holly bush, a sober lump of green,
Shines through the leafless shrubs all brown and grey,
And smiles at winter, be it e'er so keen,
With all the leafy luxury of May.
And oh, it is delicious, when the day
In winter's loaded garment keenly blows
And turns her back on sudden falling snows,
To go where gravel pathways creep between
Arches of evergreen that scarce let through
A single feather of the driving storm;
And in the bitterest day that ever blew
The walk will find some places still and warm
Where dead leaves rustle sweet and give alarm
To little birds that flirt and start away.

THE FIRST SNOW-FALL

The snow had begun in the gloaming,
    And busily all the night
Had been heaping field and highway
    With a silence deep and white.

Every pine and fir and hemlock
    Wore ermine too dear for an earl,
And the poorest twig on the elm-tree
    Was ridged inch deep with pearl.

From sheds new-roofed with Carrara
    Came Chanticleer's muffled crow,
The stiff rails softened to swan's-down,
    And still fluttered down the snow.

I stood and watched by the window
    The noiseless work of the sky,
And the sudden flurries of snow-birds,
    Like brown leaves whirling by.

I thought of a mound in sweet Auburn
    Where a little headstone stood;
How the flakes were folding it gently,
    As did robins the babes in the wood.

Up spoke our own little Mabel,
    Saying, "Father, who makes it snow?"
And I told of the good All-father
    Who cares for us here below.

Again I looked at the snow-fall,
    And thought of the leaden sky
That arched o'er our first great sorrow,
    When that mound was heaped so high.

I remembered the gradual patience
    That fell from that cloud like snow,
Flake by flake, healing and hiding
    The scar that renewed our woe.

And again to the child I whispered,
    "The snow that husheth all,
Darling, the merciful Father
    Alone can make it fall!"

Then, with eyes that saw not, I kissed her;
    And she, kissing back, could not know
That *my* kiss was given to her sister,
    Folded close under deepening snow.

JAMES RUSSELL LOWELL

FROM A NOTEBOOK

The whiteness near and far.
The cold, the hush . . .
A first word stops
The blizzard, steps
Out into fresh
Candor. You ask no more.

Each never taken stride
Leads onward, though
In circles ever
Smaller, smaller.
The vertigo
Upholds you. And now to glide

Across the frozen pond,
Steelshod, to chase
Its dreamless oval
With loop and spiral
Until (your face
Downshining, lidded, drained

Of any need to know
What hid, what called,
Wisdom or error,
Beneath that mirror)
The page you scrawled
Turns. A new day. Fresh snow.

THE SNOW-STORM

Announced by all the trumpets of the sky,
Arrives the snow, and, driving o'er the fields,
Seems nowhere to alight: the whited air
Hides hills and woods, the river, and the heaven,
And veils the farm-house at the garden's end.
The sled and traveller stopped, the courier's feet
Delayed, all friends shut out, the housemates sit
Around the radiant fireplace, enclosed
In a tumultuous privacy of storm.

Come see the north wind's masonry.
Out of an unseen quarry evermore
Furnished with tile, the fierce artificer
Curves his white bastions with projected roof
Round every windward stake, or tree, or door.
Speeding, the myriad-handed, his wild work
So fanciful, so savage, nought cares he
For number or proportion. Mockingly,
On coop or kennel he hangs Parian wreaths;
A swan-like form invests the hidden thorn;
Fills up the farmer's lane from wall to wall,
Maugre the farmer's sighs; and, at the gate,
A tapering turret overtops the work.
And when his hours are numbered, and the world
Is all his own, retiring, as he were not,

Leaves, when the sun appears, astonished Art
To mimic in slow structures, stone by stone,
Built in an age, the mad wind's night-work,
The frolic architecture of the snow.

THE PAPERWEIGHT

The scene within the paperweight is calm,
A small white house, a laughing man and wife,
Deep snow. I turn it over in my palm
And watch it snowing in another life,

Another world, and from this scene learn what
It is to stand apart: she serves him tea
Once and forever, dressed from head to foot
As she is always dressed. In this toy, history

Sifts down through the glass like snow, and we
Wonder if her single deed tells much
Or little of the way she loves, and whether he
Sees shadows in the sky. Beyond our touch,

Beyond our lives, they laugh, and drink their tea.
We look at them just as the winter night
With its vast empty spaces bends to see
Our isolated little world of light,

Covered with snow, and snow in clouds above it,
And drifts and swirls too deep to understand.
Still, I must try to think a little of it,
With so much winter in my head and hand.

From SNOW-BOUND

The sun that brief December day
Rose cheerless over hills of gray,
And, darkly circled, gave at noon
A sadder light than waning moon.
Slow tracing down the thickening sky
Its mute and ominous prophecy,
A portent seeming less than threat,
It sank from sight before it set.

A chill no coat, however stout,
Of homespun stuff could quite shut out,
A hard, dull bitterness of cold,
    That checked, mid-vein, the circling race
    Of life-blood in the sharpened face,
The coming of the snow-storm told.
The wind blew east: we heard the roar
Of Ocean on his wintry shore,
And felt the strong pulse throbbing there
Beat with low rhythm our inland air.

Meanwhile we did our nightly chores, –
Brought in the wood from out of doors,
Littered the stalls, and from the mows
Raked down the herd's-grass for the cows;
Heard the horse whinnying for his corn;

And, sharply clashing horn on horn,
Impatient down the stanchion rows
The cattle shake their walnut bows;
While, peering from his early perch
Upon the scaffold's pole of birch,
The cock his crested helmet bent
And down his querulous challenge sent.

Unwarmed by any sunset light
The gray day darkened into night,
A night made hoary with the swarm
And whirl-dance of the blinding storm,
As zigzag wavering to and fro
Crossed and recrossed the wingèd snow:
And ere the early bed-time came
The white drift piled the window-frame,
And through the glass the clothes-line posts
Looked in like tall and sheeted ghosts.

So all night long the storm roared on:
The morning broke without a sun;
In tiny spherule traced with lines
Of Nature's geometric signs,
In starry flake, and pellicle,
All day the hoary meteor fell;

And, when the second morning shone,
We looked upon a world unknown,
On nothing we could call our own.
Around the glistening wonder bent
The blue walls of the firmament,
No cloud above, no earth below, –
A universe of sky and snow!
The old familiar sights of ours
Took marvellous shapes; strange domes and towers
Rose up where sty or corn-crib stood,
Or garden wall, or belt of wood;
A smooth white mound the brush-pile showed,
A fenceless drift what once was road;
The bridle-post an old man sat
With loose-flung coat and high cocked hat;
The well-curb had a Chinese roof;
And even the long sweep, high aloof,
In its slant splendor, seemed to tell
Of Pisa's leaning miracle.

THE SNOW

Snow is in the oak.
Behind the thick, whitening
air which the wind drives,
the weight of the sun
presses the snow
on the pane of my window.

I remember snows and walking
through their first fall in cities,
asleep or drunk
with the slow, desperate falling.
The snow blurs in my eyes,
with other snows.

Snow is what must
come down, even if it struggles
to stay in the air with the strength
of the wind. Like an old man,
whatever I touch I turn
to the story of death.

Snow is what fills
the oak, and what covers
the grass and the bare garden.
Snow is what reverses

sidewalk, house and lawn
into the substance of whiteness.

So the watcher sleeps himself
back to the baby's eyes.
The tree, the breast, and the floor
are limbs of him, and from
his eyes he extends a skin
which grows over the world.

The baby is what must
have fallen, like snow. He resisted,
the way the old man
struggles inside the airy tent
to keep on breathing.
Birth is the fear of death

and the source of an old hope.
Snow is what melts. I distrust
the cycles of water.
The sun has withdrawn itself
and the snow keeps falling,
and something will always be falling.

LINES WRITTEN ON A
WINDOW AT THE LEASOWES
AT A TIME OF VERY DEEP SNOW

In this small fort, besieged with snow,
When every studious pulse beats low,
    What does my wish require?
Some sprightly girls beneath my roof,
Some friends sincere and winter-proof,
    A bottle and a fire.

Prolong, O snow, prolong thy siege!
With these, thou wilt but more oblige,
    And bless me with thy stay;
Extend, extend thy frigid reign,
My few sincerer friends detain,
    And keep false friends away.

WILLIAM SHENSTONE

SILVER FILIGREE

The icicles wreathing
   On trees in festoon
Swing, swayed to our breathing:
   They're made of the moon.

She's a pale, waxen taper;
   And these seem to drip
Transparent as paper
   From the flame of her tip.

Molten, smoking a little,
   Into crystal they pass;
Falling, freezing, to brittle
   And delicate glass.

Each a sharp-pointed flower,
   Each a brief stalactite
Which hangs for an hour
   In the blue cave of night.

TO A LEAF FALLING IN WINTER

At sundown when a day's words
have gathered at the feet of the trees
lining up in silence
to enter the long corridors
of the roots into which they
pass one by one thinking
that they remember the place
as they feel themselves climbing
away from their only sound
while they are being forgotten
by their bright circumstances
they rise through all of the rings
listening again
afterward as they
listened once and they come
to where the leaves used to live
during their lives but have gone now
and they too take the next step
beyond the reach of meaning

W. S. MERWIN

RUNES, BLURS, SAP RISING

In January, shed twigs of hemlock
leave their runic offprint of an
autograph on thawing snowbanks

whose meltwaters go down loquacious
in torques, in curdlings, cadenzas
by the earful. Today, out walking

among the evergreens – toplofty
taperers, cones, puptents – I've come
upon the guarded quiddity of how a

beech tree signs itself, in punctual
lifts, in skaterly glissandos;
how the alder neatly, minutely

rounds off each period with a
catkin's knob; and just now, in an
embrasure of the understory, this

deciduous tightrope processional,
these leaf-buds like a thing afire:
looked at up close, their quasi-

bronze a finely grooved, a paired
and pointed Asian gesture, self-
effacingly inscrutable. What

will it be? A viburnum, green
wings erupting, then a foaming
torque of bloom? No telling –

other than, come April, all
linear pronouncements will be
awash with leaf-blood's delible,
    blurred, tidal signature.

CROWS IN WINTER

Here's a meeting
of morticians in our trees.
They agree in klaxon voices:
things are looking good.
The snowfields signify
a landscape of clean skulls,
Seas of Tranquility
throughout the neighborhood.

Here's a mined,
a graven wisdom,
a bituminous air.
The first cosmetic pinks
of dawn amuse them greatly.

They foresee the expansion of graveyards,
they talk real estate.
Cras, they say,
repeating a rumor
among the whitened branches.

And the wind, a voiceless thorn,
goes over the details,
making a soft promise
to take our breath away.

SNOW-FLAKES

Out of the bosom of the Air,
    Out of the cloud-folds of her garments shaken,
Over the woodlands brown and bare,
    Over the harvest-fields forsaken,
        Silent, and soft, and slow
        Descends the snow.

Even as our cloudy fancies take
    Suddenly shape in some divine expression,
Even as the troubled heart doth make
    In the white countenance confession,
        The troubled sky reveals
        The grief it feels.

This is the poem of the air,
    Slowly in silent syllables recorded;
This is the secret of despair,
    Long in its cloudy bosom hoarded,
        Now whispered and revealed
        To wood and field.

HENRY WADSWORTH LONGFELLOW   219

AFTERFLAKES

In the thick of a teeming snowfall
I saw my shadow on snow.
I turned and looked back up at the sky,
Where we still look to ask the why
Of everything below.

If I shed such a darkness,
If the reason was in me,
That shadow of mine should show in form
Against the shapeless shadow of storm,
How swarthy I must be.

I turned and looked back upward.
The whole sky was blue;
And the thick flakes floating at a pause
Were but frost knots on an airy gauze,
With the sun shining through.

THE SNOW MAN

One must have a mind of winter
To regard the frost and the boughs
Of the pine-trees crusted with snow;

And have been cold a long time
To behold the junipers shagged with ice,
The spruces rough in the distant glitter

Of the January sun; and not to think
Of any misery in the sound of the wind,
In the sound of a few leaves,

Which is the sound of the land
Full of the same wind
That is blowing in the same bare place

For the listener, who listens in the snow,
And, nothing himself, beholds
Nothing that is not there and the nothing that is.

WALLACE STEVENS   221

"NOW WINTER NIGHTS ENLARGE"

Now winter nights enlarge
The number of their hours,
And clouds their storms discharge
Upon the airy towers.
Let now the chimneys blaze,
And cups o'erflow with wine;
Let well-tuned words amaze
With harmony divine.
Now yellow waxen lights
Shall wait on honey love,
While youthful revels, masques, and courtly sights
Sleep's leaden spells remove.

This time doth well dispense
With lovers' long discourse;
Much speech hath some defence,
Though beauty no remorse.
All do not all things well;
Some measures comely tread,
Some knotted riddles tell,
Some poems smoothly read.
The summer hath his joys
And winter his delights;
Though love and all his pleasures are but toys,
They shorten tedious nights.

A WINTER TWILIGHT

A silence slipping around like death,
Yet chased by a whisper, a sigh, a breath;
One group of trees, lean, naked and cold,
Inking their crest 'gainst a sky green-gold;
One path that knows where the corn flowers were;
Lonely, apart, unyielding, one fir;
And over it softly leaning down,
One star that I loved ere the fields went brown.

ANGELINA WELD GRIMKÉ

WINTER FEAR

Is it just winter
or is this worse.
Is this the year
when outer damp
obscures a deeper curse
that spring can't fix,
when gears that
turn the earth
won't shift the view,
when clouds won't lift
though all the skies
go blue.

SESTINA D'INVERNO

Here in this bleak city of Rochester,
Where there are twenty-seven words for "snow",
Not all of them polite, the wayward mind
Basks in some Yucatan of its own making,
Some coppery, sleek lagoon, or cinnamon island
Alive with lemon tints and burnished natives,

And O that we were there. But here the natives
Of this grey, sunless city of Rochester
Have sown whole mines of salt about their land
(Bare ruined Carthage that it is) while snow
Comes down as if The Flood were in the making.
Yet on that ocean Marvell called the mind

An ark sets forth which is itself the mind,
Bound for some pungent green, some shore whose
    natives
Blend coriander, cayenne, mint in making
Roasts that would gladden the Earl of Rochester
With sinfulness, and melt a polar snow.
It might be well to remember that an island

Was a blessed haven once, more than an island,
The grand, utopian dream of a noble mind.
In that kind climate the mere thought of snow

Was but a wedding cake; the youthful natives,
Unable to conceive of Rochester,
Made love, and were acrobatic in the making.

Dream as we may, there is far more to making
Do than some wistful reverie of an island,
Especially now when hope lies with the Rochester
Gas and Electric Co., which doesn't mind
Such profitable weather, while the natives
Sink, like Pompeians, under a world of snow.

The one thing indisputable here is snow,
The single verity of heaven's making,
Deeply indifferent to the dreams of the natives
And the torn hoarding-posters of some island.
Under our igloo skies the frozen mind
Holds to one truth: it is grey, and called Rochester.

No island fantasy survives Rochester,
Where to the natives destiny is snow
That is neither to our mind nor of our making.

WINTER SCENE

There is now not a single
leaf on the cherry tree:

except when the jay
plummets in, lights, and,

in pure clarity, squalls:
then every branch

quivers and
breaks out in blue leaves.

A. R. AMMONS

"THERE'S A CERTAIN SLANT OF LIGHT"

There's a certain Slant of light
On winter afternoons –
That oppresses, like the Heft
Of cathedral tunes.

Heavenly Hurt it gives us –
We can find no scar –
But internal difference
Where the Meanings are.

None may teach it anything
'Tis the seal, Despair –
An imperial affliction
Sent us of the air.

When it comes, the Landscape listens –
Shadows hold their breath –
When it goes, 'tis like the Distance
On the look of Death.

YEAR'S END

Now winter downs the dying of the year,
And night is all a settlement of snow;
From the soft street the rooms of houses show
A gathered light, a shapen atmosphere,
Like frozen-over lakes whose ice is thin
And still allows some stirring down within.

I've known the wind by water banks to shake
The late leaves down, which frozen where they fell
And held in ice as dancers in a spell
Fluttered all winter long into a lake;
Graved on the dark in gestures of descent,
They seemed their own most perfect monument.

There was perfection in the death of ferns
Which laid their fragile cheeks against the stone
A million years. Great mammoths overthrown
Composedly have made their long sojourns,
Like palaces of patience, in the gray
And changeless lands of ice. And at Pompeii

The little dog lay curled and did not rise
But slept the deeper as the ashes rose
And found the people incomplete, and froze
The random hands, the loose unready eyes

Of men expecting yet another sun
To do the shapely thing they had not done.

These sudden ends of time must give us pause.
We fray into the future, rarely wrought
Save in the tapestries of afterthought.
More time, more time. Barrages of applause
Come muffled from a buried radio.
The New-year bells are wrangling with the snow.

SNOW AND SNOW

Snow is sometimes a she, a soft one.
   Her kiss on your cheek, her finger on your sleeve
In early December, on a warm evening,
     And you turn to meet her, saying "It's snowing!"
       But it is not. And nobody's there.
       Empty and calm is the air.

Sometimes the snow is a he, a sly one.
   Weakly he signs the dry stone with a damp spot.
Waifish he floats and touches the pond and is not.
     Treacherous-beggarly he falters, and taps at the
         window.
       A little longer he clings to the grass-blade tip
       Getting his grip.

Then how she leans, how furry foxwrap she nestles
    The sky with her warm, and the earth with her
        softness.
How her lit crowding fairytales sink through the
        space-silence
    To build her palace, till it twinkles in starlight –
       Too frail for a foot
       Or a crumb of soot.

Then how his muffled armies move in all night
  And we wake and every road is blockaded
Every hill taken and every farm occupied
  And the white glare of his tents is on the ceiling.
    And all that dull blue day and on into the gloaming
    We have to watch more coming.

Then everything in the rubbish-heaped world
  Is a bridesmaid at her miracle.
Dunghills and crumbly dark old barns are bowed in
    the chapel of her sparkle,
  The gruesome boggy cellars of the wood
    Are a wedding of lace
    Now taking place.

"THE NIGHT IS DARKENING ROUND ME"

The night is darkening round me,
The wild winds coldly blow;
But a tyrant spell has bound me
And I cannot, cannot go.

The giant trees are bending
Their bare boughs weighed with snow.
And the storm is fast descending,
And yet I cannot go.

Clouds beyond clouds above me,
Wastes beyond wastes below;
But nothing drear can move me;
I will not, cannot go.

EMILY BRONTË

STOPPING BY WOODS ON
A SNOWY EVENING

Whose woods these are I think I know.
His house is in the village though;
He will not see me stopping here
To watch his woods fill up with snow.

My little horse must think it queer
To stop without a farmhouse near
Between the woods and frozen lake
The darkest evening of the year.

He gives his harness bells a shake
To ask if there is some mistake.
The only other sound's the sweep
Of easy wind and downy flake.

The woods are lovely, dark and deep,
But I have promises to keep,
And miles to go before I sleep,
And miles to go before I sleep.

CALIFORNIA WINTER

It is winter in California, and outside
Is like the interior of a florist shop:
A chilled and moisture-laden crop
Of pink camellias lines the path; and what
Rare roses for a banquet or a bride,
So multitudinous that they seem a glut!

A line of snails crosses the golf-green lawn
From the rosebushes to the ivy bed;
An arsenic compound is distributed
For them. The gardener will rake up the shells
And leave in a corner of the patio
The little mound of empty snails, like skulls.

By noon the fog is burnt off by the sun
And the world's immensest sky opens a page
For the exercises of a future age;
Now jet planes draw straight lines, parabolas,
And x's, which the wind, before they're done,
Erases leisurely or pulls to fuzz.

It is winter in the valley of the vine.
The vineyards crucified on stakes suggest
War cemeteries, but the fruit is pressed,
The redwood vats are brimming in the shed,

And on the sidings stand tank cars of wine,
For which bright juice a billion grapes have bled.

And skiers from the snow line driving home
Descend through almond orchards, olive farms,
Fig tree and palm tree – everything that warms
The imagination of the wintertime.
If the walls were older one would think of Rome:
If the land were stonier one would think of Spain.

But this land grows the oldest living things,
Trees that were young when Pharaohs ruled the
    world,
Trees whose new leaves are only just unfurled.
Beautiful they are not; they oppress the heart
With gigantism and with immortal wings;
And yet one feels the sumptuousness of this dirt.

It is raining in California, a straight rain
Cleaning the heavy oranges on the bough,
Filling the gardens till the gardens flow,
Shining the olives, tiling the gleaming tile,
Waxing the dark camellia leaves more green,
Flooding the daylong valleys like the Nile.

WINTER

Now the snow
lies on the ground
and more snow
is descending upon it –
Patches of red dirt
hold together
the old
snow patches

This is winter –
rosettes of
leather-green leaves
by the old fence
and bare trees
marking the sky –

This is winter
winter, winter
leather-green leaves
spearshaped
in the falling snow

WILLIAM CARLOS WILLIAMS   237

"THE SKY IS LOW – THE CLOUDS ARE MEAN"

The Sky is low – the Clouds are mean.
A Travelling Flake of Snow
Across a Barn or through a Rut
Debates if it will go –

A Narrow Wind complains all Day
How some one treated him;
Nature, like Us is sometimes caught
Without her Diadem.

ORCHARD TREES, JANUARY

It's not the case, though some might wish it so
Who from a window watch the blizzard blow

White riot through their branches vague and stark,
That they keep snug beneath their pelted bark.

They take affliction in until it jells
To crystal ice between their frozen cells,

And each of them is inwardly a vault
Of jewels rigorous and free of fault,

Unglimpsed by us until in May it bears
A sudden crop of green-pronged solitaires.

RICHARD WILBUR

FEBRUARY AFTERNOON

Men heard this roar of parleying starlings, saw,
    A thousand years ago even as now,
    Black rooks with white gulls following the plough
So that the first are last until a caw
Commands that last are first again, – a law
    Which was of old when one, like me, dreamed how
    A thousand years might dust lie on his brow
Yet thus would birds do between hedge and shaw.

Time swims before me, making as a day
    A thousand years, while the broad ploughland oak
    Roars mill-like and men strike and bear the stroke
    Of war as ever, audacious or resigned,
And God still sits aloft in the array
    That we have wrought him, stone-deaf and
        stone-blind.

FEBRUARY 13, 1975

Tomorrow is St. Valentine's:
tomorrow I'll think about
that. Always nervous, even
after a good sleep I'd like
to climb back into. The sun
shines on yesterday's new-
fallen snow and yestereven
it turned the world to pink
and rose and steel-blue
buildings. Helene is restless:
leaving soon. And what then
will I do with myself? Some-
one is watching morning
TV. I'm not reduced to that
yet. I wish one could press
snowflakes in a book like flowers.

INDEX OF AUTHORS

246

247

ACKNOWLEDGMENTS

ADAMS, LÉONIE: "Midsummer" by Léonie Adams, from *Poems* (Funk & Wagnalls, 1954, p. 105). AMMONS, A. R.: "Winter Scene". Copyright © 1965 by A. R. Ammons, from *Collected Poems 1951–1971* by A. R. Ammons. Used by permission of W. W. Norton & Company, Inc. "Late November" and "Resurrections" from *The Really Short Poems of A. R. Ammons* by A. R. Ammons. Copyright © 1990 by A. R. Ammons. Used by permission of W. W. Norton & Company, Inc. BISHOP, ELIZABETH: "A Cold Spring" from *The Complete Poems 1927–1979* by Elizabeth Bishop. Copyright © 1979, 1983 by Alice Helen Methfessel. Reprinted by permission of Farrar, Straus and Giroux, LLC. BOGAN, LOUISE: "Simple Autumnal" from *The Blue Estuaries* by Louise Bogan. Copyright © 1968 by Louise Bogan. Copyright renewed 1996 by Ruth Limmer. Reprinted by permission of Farrar, Straus and Giroux, LLC. CLAMPITT, AMY: "Lindenbloom" and "Runes, Blurs, Sap Rising" from *The Collected Poems of Amy Clampitt* by Amy Clampitt, copyright © 1997 by the Estate of Amy Clampitt. Introduction copyright © 1997 by Mary Jo Slater. Used by permission of Alfred A. Knopf, a division of Random House, Inc. CUMMINGS, E. E.: "in Just-". Copyright 1923, 1951, © 1991 by the Trustees for the E. E. Cummings Trust. Copyright © 1976 by George James Firmage. "I (a". Copyright © 1958, 1986, 1991 by the Trustees for the E. E. Cummings Trust. From *Complete Poems: 1904–1962* by E. E. Cummings, edited by George J. Firmage. Used by permission of Liveright Publishing Corporation. DE LA MARE, WALTER: "Autumn" from *The Complete Poems of Walter de la Mare*. Reprinted with permission from The Literary Trustees of Walter de la Mare and The Society of Authors as their representative. DICKINSON, EMILY: "A Light exists in Spring" and "The Sky is low – the Clouds are mean". Reprinted by permission of the publishers and the Trustees of Amherst College from *The Poems of Emily Dickinson*, Thomas H. Johnson, ed., Cambridge, Mass.: The Belknap Press of Harvard University Press, Copyright © 1951, 1955, 1979, 1983 by the President and Fellows of Harvard College. FROST, ROBERT: "Nothing Gold Can Stay", "Spring Pools", "Putting in the Seed", "Hyla Brook", "Unharvested", "Afterflakes", "Stopping by Woods on a Snowy Evening" from *The Poetry of Robert Frost* edited by Edward Connery Lathem, published by Jonathan Cape, reprinted by permission of The Random House Group Limited. "Nothing Gold Can Stay", "Spring Pools", "Putting in the Seed", "Hyla Brook", "Unharvested", "Afterflakes", "Stopping by Woods on a Snowy Evening" from *The Poetry of Robert Frost* edited by Edward Connery Lathem. Copyright 1916, 1923, 1928, 1969 by Henry Holt and Company, copyright 1936, 1944, 1951, 1956 by Robert Frost, copyright 1964 by Lesley Frost Ballantine. Reprinted by arrangement with Henry Holt and Company. GARRIGUE, JEAN: "Spring Song II" and "The Flux of Autumn" by Jean Garrigue. Reprinted by permission of The Estate of Jean Garrigue. GRIMKÉ, ANGELINA WELD: "A Winter Twilight" by Angelina Grimké. Reprinted by kind permission of Moorland Spingarn Research Center. HALL, DONALD: "The Snow" from *Old and New Poems* by Donald Hall. Copyright © 1990 by Donald Hall. Reprinted by permission of Houghton Mifflin Company. All rights reserved. HEANEY, SEAMUS: "Blackberry-Picking" from *Death of a Naturalist* by Seamus Heaney. Reprinted with permission from Faber & Faber Limited. "Blackberry-Picking" from *Opened Ground: Selected Poems 1966–1996* by Seamus Heaney. Copyright © 1998 by Seamus Heaney. Reprinted by permission of Farrar, Straus and Giroux, LLC. HECHT, ANTHONY: "An Autumnal" and "Sestina d'Inverno" from *Collected Earlier Poems* by Anthony Hecht, copyright © 1990 by Anthony E. Hecht. Used by permission of Alfred A. Knopf, a division of

Random House, Inc. and Carcanet Press Limited. "Crows in Winter" from *Collected Later Poems* by Anthony Hecht, copyright © 2003 by Anthony Hecht. Used by permission of Alfred A. Knopf, a division of Random House, Inc. HOLLANDER, JOHN: "Late August on the Lido" from *Selected Poetry* by John Hollander, copyright © 1993 by John Hollander. Used by permission of Alfred A. Knopf, a division of Random House, Inc. "An Old-Fashioned Song" from *Tesserae and Other Poems* by John Hollander, copyright © 1993 by John Hollander. Used by permission of Alfred A. Knopf, a division of Random House, Inc. HUGHES, LANGSTON: "Summer Night" edited by Arnold Rampersad with David Roessel, Assoc., from *The Collected Poems of Langston Hughes* by Langston Hughes, edited by Arnold Rampersad with David Roessel, Associate Editor, copyright © 1994 by the Estate of Langston Hughes. Used by permission of Alfred A. Knopf, a division of Random House, Inc. and by permission of David Higham Associates, London. HUGHES, TED: "March Morning Unlike Others" and "Heatwave" from *Moortown Songs*; "The Seven Sorrows" and "Snow and Snow" from *Season Songs*; "October Dawn" from *The Hawk in the Rain* by Ted Hughes. Reprinted with permission from Faber & Faber Limited. "Heatwave", "March Morning Unlike Others", "October Dawn", "The Seven Sorrows" and "Snow and Snow" from *Collected Poems* by Ted Hughes. Copyright © 2003 by The Estate of Ted Hughes. Reprinted by permission of Farrar, Straus and Giroux, LLC. MCGINLEY, PHYLLIS: "June in the Suburbs" copyright 1953 by Phyllis McGinley, "November" copyright 1937 by Phyllis McGinley, from *Three Times* by Phyllis McGinley. Used by permission of Viking Penguin, a division of Penguin Group (USA) Inc. "June in the Suburbs" and "November" from *Three Times* by Phyllis McGinley, published by Secker and Warburg. Reprinted by permission of The Random House Group Limited. MERRILL, JAMES: "From a Notebook" and "Another April" from

Collected Poems by James Merrill and J. D. McClatchy and Stephen Yenser, editors, copyright © 2001 by the Literary Estate of James Merrill at Washington University. Used by permission of Alfred A. Knopf, a division of Random House, Inc. MERWIN, W. S.: "The Love for October" by W. S. Merwin. © by W. S. Merwin, permission of The Wylie Agency. "To a Falling Leaf in Winter" by W. S. Merwin, from *Present Company* (Copper Canyon Press, 2005, p.100). MILLAY, EDNA ST VINCENT: "Autumn Chant" by Edna St Vincent Millay. Taken from *The Harp-Weaver and Other Poems* (Harper, 1923). NEMEROV, HOWARD: "Trees" and "The Dying Garden" by Howard Nemerov. Reprinted by permission of Margaret Nemerov. OLIVER, MARY: "Spring" ("This morning...") from *West Wind: Poems and Prose Poems* by Mary Oliver. Copyright © 1997 by Mary Oliver. Reprinted by permission of Houghton Mifflin Company. All rights reserved. "Summer Poem" from *What Do We Know?* by Mary Oliver. Reprinted by permission of Da Capo Press, a member of Perseus Books Group. "Spring" ("Somewhere...") from *New and Selected Poems* by Mary Oliver (Beacon, 1992). Reprinted with permission from Beacon Press. PONSOT, MARIE: "End of October" from *Springing: New and Selected Poems* by Marie Ponsot, copyright © 2002 by Marie Ponsot. Used by permission of Alfred A. Knopf, a division of Random House, Inc. PUSHKIN, ALEXANDER: From 'A Pushkin Portfolio' in *Modern Poetry in Translation* (New Series, no 15), 1999, published by King's College, London. Reprinted with the permission of Antony Wood (translator). REED, HENRY: "Naming of Parts" (30 lines) from *Lessons of War* from *Collected Poems* by Reed, Henry, edited by Stallworthy, Jon (1991). By permission of Oxford University Press. RYAN, KAY: "Sonnet to Spring" from *Elephant Rocks* by Kay Ryan. Copyright © 1996 by Kay Ryan. Used by permission of Grove/Atlantic, Inc. "Winter Fear" from *Say Uncle* by Kay Ryan. Copyright © 2000 by Kay Ryan. Used by permission of Grove/

Atlantic, Inc. SCHNACKENBERG, GJERTRUD: "The Paperweight" by
Gjertrud Schnackenberg, from *Supernatural Love: Poems 1976–
2000* (Bloodaxe Books, 2001). Reprinted with permission from
Bloodaxe Books. "The Paperweight" from *Supernatural Love:
Poems 1976–2000* by Gjertrud Schnackenberg. Copyright © 2000
by Gjertrud Schnackenberg. Reprinted by permission of Farrar,
Straus and Giroux, LLC. SCHUYLER, JAMES: "I Think" and "Febru-
ary 13, 1975" from *Collected Poems* by James Schuyler. Copyright
© 1993 by the Estate of James Schuyler. Reprinted by permission
of Farrar, Straus and Giroux, LLC. SHAPIRO, KARL: "California
Winter" by Karl Shapiro. Reprinted by permission of Harold Ober
Associates, Incorporated. Copyright © 1968 by Karl Shapiro.
SMITH, STEVIE: "Black March" by Stevie Smith. Reprinted by per-
mission of the Executors of James MacGibbon. STEVENS, WALLACE:
"Autumn Refrain", "The House was Quiet and the World was
Calm" and "The Snow Man", copyright 1923 and renewed 1951
by Wallace Stevens, from *The Collected Poems of Wallace Stevens* by
Wallace Stevens, copyright 1954 by Wallace Stevens and renewed
1982 by Holly Stevens. Used by permission of Alfred A. Knopf, a
division of Random House, Inc. "Autumn Refrain", "The House
was Quiet and the World was Calm" and "The Snow Man" from
Collected Poems by Wallace Stevens. Reprinted by permission of
Faber & Faber Limited. SWENSON, MAY: "April Light" and "Flag of
Summer" from *Nature: Poems Old and New* by May Swenson.
Copyright © 1994 by The Literary Estate of May Swen-
son. Reprinted by permission of Houghton Mifflin Company. All
rights reserved. VAN DUYN, MONA: "End of May" from *Selected
Poems* by Mona Van Duyn, copyright © 2002 by Mona Van Duyn.
Used by permission of Alfred A. Knopf, a division of Random
House, Inc. WAGONER, DAVID: "Falling Asleep in a Garden" by
David Wagoner, from *Travelling Light: Collected and New Poems.*
Copyright 1999 by David Wagoner. Used with permission of the

University of Illinois Press and David Wagoner. WARREN, ROBERT PENN: "August Moon" and "Heart of Autumn" by Robert Penn Warren. Taken from *Being Here: Poetry 1977–1980* (Random House, 1980, pp. 31–2). WILBUR, RICHARD: "March" from *The Mind-Reader*, copyright © 1971 and renewed 1999 by Richard Wilbur, reprinted by permission of Harcourt, Inc. "A Storm in April" from *The Mind-Reader*, copyright © 1973 by Richard Wilbur, reprinted by permission of Harcourt, Inc. "Orchard Trees, January" from *Ceremony and Other Poems*, copyright © 1982 by Richard Wilbur, reprinted by permission of Harcourt, Inc. "Year's End" from *Ceremony and Other Poems*, copyright © 1949 and renewed 1977 by Richard Wilbur, reprinted by permission of Harcourt, Inc. "My Father Paints the Summer" from *The Beautiful Changes and Other Poems*, copyright © 1947 and renewed 1975 by Richard Wilbur, reprinted by permission of Harcourt, Inc. "Crow's Nests" from *Mayflies: New Poems and Translations*, copyright © 2000 by Richard Wilbur, reprinted by permission of Harcourt, Inc. "March", "A Storm in April", "Orchard Trees, January", "Year's End", "My Father Paints the Summer" and "Crow's Nests" from *New and Selected Poems* by Richard Wilbur. Reprinted by permission of Faber & Faber Limited. WILLIAMS, WILLIAM CARLOS: "The Widow's Lament in Springtime" and "Winter" by William Carlos Williams, from *Collected Poems*. Reprinted with permission from Carcanet Press Limited. "The Widow's Lament in Springtime" and "Winter" by William Carlos Williams, from *Collected Poems: 1909–1939*, Volume I, copyright © 1938 by New Directions Publishing Corp. Reprinted by permission of New Directions Publishing Corp.

Although every effort has been made to trace and contact copyright holders, in a few instances this has not been possible. If notified, the publishers will be pleased to rectify any omission in future editions.